LEVERAGING EMOTIONAL INTELLIGENCE

YOUR BLUEPRINT FOR LIFELONG LEARNING, MEANINGFUL CONNECTIONS, AND PERSONAL TRANSFORMATION

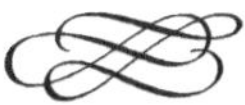

R.J. ATKINS

CONTENTS

INTRODUCTION

We've all heard of Nikola Tesla, Albert Einstein, and Stephen Hawking, who all had IQ scores of over 160. If the world were a toolshed, they would be the sharpest tools of the bunch. Don't you agree? But what exactly is IQ, and what does it have to do with the brightest minds this world has ever known?

IQ stands for intelligence quotient and measures how good someone is at solving for x, understanding how a raven is like a writing desk, and what exactly e=mc^2 actually means. The lower someone's IQ is, the more difficult it will be for them to understand the "smart stuff" that those with higher IQ scores seem to grasp immediately. This smart stuff includes stuff like mathematics, science, physics, biology, etc. And, in a world advancing through mathematical, scientific, and medical discoveries, breakthroughs, and inventions, people with high IQ scores are invaluable!

However, there is another aspect of the human psyche that is just as valuable as IQ, even if it is less famously known.

EQ stands for emotional quotient and measures how good someone is at recognizing and understanding the emotions of those around them, as well as themselves. The term I will be using in this book, however, is emotional intelligence, or EI. EI is a term that is mostly used interchangeably with EQ. It is a term that was popularized by Dr. Daniel Goleman in 1995, and, similarly to EQ, it is the ability to identify, comprehend, and manage or influence one's own emotions and the emotions of others (Institute for Health and Human Potential, n.d.-b).

In a world with over eight billion people—at the time of writing—each with their own unique and complex emotions, you can imagine how helpful a high EI score could be. In fact, salespeople with high EQ scores are proven to be capable of producing twice the revenue of their colleagues with lower scores. Furthermore, compared to those with lower scores, technical programmers in the top 10% of EQ scores were able to produce software three times faster and with higher quality (Hay Group, 2011).

In my life, I have met many people with a wide range of IQ and EQ scores. I have found that so often, those with lower IQ scores feel as if they are inadequate, unimportant, or even stupid. On the flip side, however, I have also found that people with lower EI scores feel the same way! See, there are plenty of resources on how to better understand math and science, but learning how to understand and recognize emotions is significantly more difficult. Math and science are fairly predictable, and when there is room for spontaneity, we can make calculated guesses. But people are far more unpredictable and erratic. It is not as easy as recognizing that furrowed eyebrows mean that someone is angry. Each person reacts to and expresses anger in a different way and lets that anger define their behavior in different ways. And having a lower EI can cause more problems than you might initially think.

Not being able to fully recognize or interact with the emotions of those around you can significantly affect the way you communicate with them. Communication is a crucial life skill that plays a role in every significant aspect of one's life. People communicate with their partners, colleagues, bosses, children, strangers, and even themselves on a daily basis, and how they choose to communicate is a key determinant of how situations will play out.

An important part of good communication is relating to—or at least respecting—the emotions of the other person. Not being able to do that can have negative ramifications. You may come across as insensitive, unapproachable, or rude, even if you never intended to be. You may experience people saying, "You just don't get it." You may hear the phrase "I was clearly [sad, angry, upset, etc.]" and feel like it wasn't that *clear* to you. Beyond this, you may miss out on opportunities due to this inability to communicate effectively.

These opportunities may include possible team collaborations or leadership and management roles. Not only will you struggle to maintain the authority and respect that a leader and fellow team members require, but you may also struggle to motivate and inspire positive relationships, working environments, and results. Being unable to do these things puts you at a big disadvantage in terms of promotions in the workplace, even if, technically and academically, you are well qualified.

Much of this miscommunication comes from a person's inability to understand or empathize with other people's emotions. Even if someone is able to identify someone else's emotions, it doesn't necessarily translate to understanding that emotion. While you may recognize that your partner is angry, you may still struggle to understand why they're angry or empathize with that emotion. Perhaps the situation that upset them is not something that would have angered you, and therefore, you can't understand why they let it upset them. Incidents like that, especially if they are regular occurrences, can lead to the failure of relationships and friendships. No one wants to live life completely alone, and it's worse when the "problem" seems like something that is unfixable.

But please know that

- you are not broken.
- it is fixable.

Understanding and leveraging your emotional intelligence is a great way to overcome these obstacles and shortcomings. Just like IQ, your EI is possible to hone, train, and improve.

I've spent a lot of my life dealing with human beings who are notorious for being unable to recognize and respect emotions: children. Using the knowledge I gained by achieving a bachelor's degree in elementary education, a master's degree in reading and curriculum instruction, and one in human resources, I spent 15 years teaching children in underprivileged communities. But, surprisingly, it was not my time with children that gave me a passion for emotional intelligence. See, I come from a family of leaders, and I now coach teachers and instructional coaches. It was in my interactions with adults that I realized emotional intelligence is not a trait that

- everyone was taught.
- can only be taught to children.

See, adults need help to use and understand their emotional intelligence to their own advantage. And, in my experience, people using their emotional intelligence is something that, by proxy, benefits those around them as well.

Beyond understanding the emotions of others and being able to interact with them appropriately and sympathetically, EI can help someone understand and manage their own emotions in a much more efficient and productive way.

People with lower EI scores struggle to recognize and understand their own emotions as much as they do other people's. And while that may sound like something that is not too big of a deal, it can have horrible consequences. Being unable to identify your own emotions can lead to bottling up those emotions and being unable to regulate and control those emotions. This lack of control and regulation can lead to outbursts of aggression, depression, and panic attacks, among others, some of which can hurt those around you as much as yourself.

Being able to acknowledge our own emotions can help us regulate them better. Being able to recognize that you are angry in a situation can help you prevent yourself from getting worked up or doing and/or saying something you'll regret later. Something as simple as saying, "I need a moment to calm down," can de-escalate the tension in a situation and help avoid irrevocable damage.

Considering the incredible importance and advantages of emotional intelligence, I feel that this is a topic that requires and deserves proper discussion and education. You *can* learn emotional intelligence. You can access the benefits of having a higher EI. And I wrote this book to help you do that. I wrote this book for people like me—for people who no longer want to feel like they can't control their own emotions. I wrote this book for those of you who have made mistakes because you misread a room, for those of you who have been told you're insensitive, and for those of you who simply want to be a more empathic and sensitive person.

My goal and my hope for this book is that, by the end, you will have a better understanding of what emotional intelligence is and how to use it in your life for the betterment of your own mental health and relationships. The skills you will learn in this book will help you with

- **Empathy.** Empathy is the ability to take the emotions of those around you into consideration and see things from their perspective. This is beneficial in relationships, friendships, with colleagues, and even with clients.
- **Self-awareness.** Self-awareness is the ability to identify your own strengths, weaknesses, feelings, emotional triggers, values, motivations, and goals. This is beneficial in relation to regulating your own behavior and reactions.
- **Self-management.** Self-management is the ability to control and regulate your emotions. This is beneficial in terms of anger management, stress control, and avoiding impulsive behaviors.
- **Relationship management.** Relationship management is the ability to build and maintain interpersonal relationships with the people you interact with on a daily basis. This is incredibly beneficial in relationships, friendships, with colleagues, and with clients.
- **Motivation.** Much of our behavior is driven by motivation. We do things we are motivated to do, and we don't do things we aren't motivated to do. However, realistically, we sometimes have to do things, even when we're unmotivated. Knowing how to motivate yourself can make those tasks much less of a mountain to climb.

So, as you read this book, I hope your passion for emotional intelligence grows the way mine has over the years. I hope that this book can act as a blueprint for you and that you reference it whenever you need a strategy—whenever you need guidance—for dealing with your emotions and the emotions of others. Hear my heart when I say that I truly want you to succeed. My desire is for this book to transform you and add value to your life.

UNDERSTANDING EMOTIONS FIRST

Over the years, there has been the ongoing concept of "heart versus head." Whenever we are faced with tough decisions or challenges in our lives, we often have to consider whether we will listen to our hearts or our heads. In other words, we must decide whether or not we will let our emotions or logical reasoning drive our actions forward. The problem with this idea is that, usually, it is far easier to decipher what's going on in our heads than what's going on in our hearts.

If we're in a difficult situation, it isn't difficult to know that quitting a job means you're out of a paycheck. It isn't difficult to know that leaving a relationship means you might have to move back in with your parents. Often, our minds are focused not only on the consequences of whatever decision we make but also on the necessary steps to follow through on that decision.

Our hearts, however, are far more complex to decipher, and even when we can decipher them, it's not always easy to know what decision that emotion is leading us to make. For this reason, before we talk about emotional intelligence, we must gain an understanding of emotions themselves.

WHAT ARE EMOTIONS?

Experiencing emotions is complicated and complex. Defining emotions, just as much. The easiest way to do so is to break it down into its three major components.

- **Subjective experience**

Unsurprisingly, emotions are considered to be highly personal and subjective. How I experience and express an emotion is most likely different than how you would experience and express the same emotion. There is a general consensus around what the basic emotions feel like (more on that later), but your own life experience can have a significant effect on even those. More often than not, we aren't just feeling one basic emotion. As complex human beings, we are often feeling a mix of several different emotions at once. The best example of this is how excitement and anxiety often come as a package deal—think of the last time you had a job interview. Though you were thrilled about the opportunity, you were anxious about making a good impression.

- **Physiological response**

I have a weird reaction to anxiety. When I am feeling particularly nervous, not only do I get nauseated, but my kneecaps start shaking like crazy. I have no control over this. My sister has a different reaction to anxiety—she starts to struggle with shortness of breath and dizziness. Our bodies react to our emotions, even if we don't know we're feeling them. This is an autonomic nervous system response, and it is responsible for controlling our flight-or-fight response. We may not even register that we're feeling unsafe, but our bodies will register and react immediately.

- **Behavioral response**

This is how we express our emotions. This is different for each person, and it is also our best resource for interpreting how other people are feeling. We cannot observe their subjective or physiological response, but we can observe their behavioral response. Behavioral responses are also the only component that can be externally influenced. How we are taught or encouraged to express our emotions may play a role. Our culture may also play a role, as Eastern and Western cultures promote and value different expressions of emotion.

Types of Emotions

As mentioned above, there is a general consensus on how the six basic or primary emotions are experienced. Paul Eckman was the man responsible for identifying what these six basic or primary emotions are. He theorized that regardless of culture, there are six basic or primary human emotions that everyone on the planet feels (Cherry, 2022b).

- sadness
- joy
- anger
- disgust
- fear
- surprise

However, we know that emotions are anything but basic. I don't see nervousness, jealousy, or guilt on that list, and I know that those are common emotions as well. Well, other scientists have expanded on the emotion theory to include secondary emotions or combined emotions.

A psychologist named Robert Plutchik proposed a "color wheel of emotions," where primary emotions or colors could combine in many different ways to create new emotions or colors. More recent studies suggest that rather than feeling one emotion at a time, people experience emotions on a gradient where one emotion can mingle and slip into the next effortlessly (Cherry, 2022b).

Having an understanding of these theories really helps me put my emotions into perspective, and I hope it does the same for you. At the end of the day, I can now almost track how my mood shifted throughout the day. Previously, the most I could recognize was that my day started off on a good note and got progressively worse. Now, I am able to say I was cheery at breakfast but became stressed at work and got progressively more overwhelmed with work until I got home, and I am now exhausted and irritable.

This is part of emotional intelligence—just having more knowledge about what emotions are and how they work.

EMOTIONS VS. FEELINGS

Most of us use the terms "feelings" and "emotions" interchangeably —well, as far as the laws of grammar and syntax allow us to. However, despite conveying the same concept, the two words mean two completely different things.

The main difference between the two is the level of consciousness we have over them. *Emotions* are entirely subconscious. Emotions are bodily reactions created by hormone releases and neurotransmitters.

Feelings, on the other hand, are the more—but not entirely—conscious experience of those emotional reactions. Feelings are only initiated by emotions, but they are sculpted by our personal experiences, memories, beliefs, and thoughts.

In other words, a feeling is the result of your brain perceiving and making sense of an emotion.

EMOTIONAL TRIGGERS

Emotions are not random. More often than not, they are externally triggered. Being influenced by the world around us is a natural part of being human. During a person's life, they will most likely experience many painful things. As adults, things that remind us—even subconsciously—of those painful experiences can trigger an emotional response.

Common emotional triggers include:

- rejection
- insecurities
- loss (of people, opportunities, control, or life circumstances)
- unfair treatment
- being blamed or shamed
- criticism, judgment, or disapproval
- helplessness
- betrayal
- being ignored or excluded
- feeling unneeded or unwanted

- the pressure of being too needed or smothered
- abandonment (or threat thereof)

Now, we cannot control the things that happen around us. There is no surefire way to make sure we aren't ever triggered. However, learning what our emotional triggers are can play a huge part in helping us regulate our emotions. Once we understand which events trigger us, we are in a better position to handle the emotions that come up.

Later in this book, we will learn how to do exactly that.

ANATOMY OF HUMAN EMOTIONS

Unfortunately, there is nothing on this beautiful earth that isn't defined or somehow affected by the "smart stuff." Emotions are no exception to this. Even emotions have a "smart stuff" explanation.

As with anything regarding the human body and experience, we cannot talk about emotions without talking about the brain. Even the heart is influenced by the head. In fact, the head is responsible for the heart—both literally and figuratively.

As with most things, there is a group of brain structures that are responsible for emotions. While the full list of structures is unclear, there are a few that are well-accepted as part of the team.

- The amygdala is responsible for taking in emotional triggers and coordinating the body's response. It plays a role in fear, anger, and motivation.
- The insula is responsible for disgust. It is the reason we gag at the sight of mold on bread and know not to put it in our mouths.

- The periaqueductal gray is responsible for recognizing pain and may be part of the reason we're able to distract ourselves from feeling pain. It is responsible for pain perception, defensive behaviors, maternal attachments, and even anxiety.
- The limbic cortex is composed of both the parahippocampal gyrus and the cingulate gyrus and is responsible for mood, judgment, and motivation.
- Memories are stored in and retrieved from the hippocampus.
- The hypothalamus governs emotional responses and hormonal, sexual, and bodily reactions.

HORMONES INFLUENCING EMOTIONS

The main role of the brain in controlling emotions is hormone release. Hormones are another one of those "smart things" that can be complex to understand. In fact, there is an entire medical field dedicated to studying hormones called endocrinology. I won't be going into the nitty-gritty here because, unfortunately, my resume does not include a degree in endocrinology.

However, I do believe that having a basic idea of how it works can offer us better insight into how our emotions work. The key to hormones, I've discovered, is that we want them to be balanced. Too little or too much of any hormone is bound to stir up an emotional mess.

1. **The lack of serotonin and dopamine.** These two hormones are often referred to as the "happy hormones." Without adequate levels of either, there is a significant risk of depression. Factors that contribute to our serotonin and

dopamine levels include liver health, sugar levels, and conditions such as hepatitis, diabetes, and insulin resistance.

2. **The lack of thyroid hormones.** Thyroid hormones stimulate cell function, and when they are missing, we can become depressed and fatigued.

3. **The lack of testosterone.** Many of the organs in our body have testosterone receptors that need to be regularly activated in order to function correctly. When there is a lack of testosterone, it can lead to fatigue, depression, and a low sex drive.

4. **The overproduction of estrogen.** Similar to testosterone, estrogen is responsible for the proper function of many organs in the body. When there is an imbalance, it can lead to many uncomfortable symptoms, such as bloating and breast tenderness, as well as headaches, lower sex drive, and mood swings.

STAGES OF EMOTIONAL DEVELOPMENT

Now, it's no secret that children aren't the most emotionally sensitive beings in the world. You won't believe the kind of things your kids spill to their teachers about you. They really say the darndest things, especially in moments when adults might have been a bit more delicate. Because of this, I am sure that none of you are surprised to learn that emotions develop over time and that we are not born with the ability to recognize and control emotions.

From the time a child is born to their fifth birthday, they go through three major stages of emotional development. These three stages are the building blocks upon which the rest of our emotional development and intelligence are built.

Stage 1: Noticing emotions. This happens between birth and the age of one. In learning the new world around them, babies will soon find that mama's cuddles feel good and an empty stomach feels bad. At its core, this is infants learning how different things make them feel.

Stage 2: Expressing emotions. This happens between two and three years of age. Ever heard of the Terrible Twos? In a big way, the tantrums and outbursts that this stage is infamous for are really instances of toddlers expressing their big emotions. As children grow more independent and cognitive of the world around them, they experiment with different ways of expressing their emotions in that world.

Stage 3: Managing emotions. This happens between three and five years of age. During this stage, children are being exposed to other children and spend prolonged periods of time away from their parents. This is a huge opportunity for growth and for developing new coping skills for managing those big emotions.

MOVING ONTO THE INTELLIGENCE BIT

Now, let's talk about the head. It's not usually what we're encouraged to follow. Rarely have I ever seen a daytime movie where the lesson was "follow your head and be logical." No. We're always told to follow our hearts and trust our emotions, but never to let them control us.

In my experience, both the head and the heart are necessary. You cannot have one without the other. It is a well-established fact that the head influences the heart, and we'd be fools to assume the opposite isn't true. Not only are both head and heart necessary, but gaining an understanding of one can give us better insight into the other. It is no coincidence that the central theme of this entire book is a combination of both head and heart: emotional intelligence.

So, let us briefly explore the concept of intelligence, and then we can address the elephant in the room.

WHAT IS INTELLIGENCE?

Much like emotion, the definition of intelligence is a complex concept to define precisely. Based on my research, there are conflicting opinions on the official definition of intelligence. Some think it's about the ability to think before acting. Some think it's about understanding and being able to gain knowledge. Since the birth of psychology, different scholars have been forming their own opinions on what exactly intelligence is and what it encompasses.

However, there is a general consensus on the basic components of intelligence and the different types of intelligence that exist.

Intelligence is defined as the ability to

- think.
- learn or gain new knowledge.
- understand.
- put new knowledge to use.

In the introduction to this book, I made mention of Tesla, Einstein, and Hawking. In this section, I beg you to consider whether other bright minds, such as Stan Lee and Winston Churchill, are any more or less intelligent than them. What about minds like Steven Spielberg or Martin Luther King Jr.?

I think you'd be hard-pressed to say that any of these men were less intelligent than the "big three," and they were by no means less well-known. They were vessels of different types of intelligence. See, there are three main types of intelligence:

- **Analytical intelligence:** (Also known as academic intelligence) It is characterized by the ability to judge, compare, and analyze information. You often see this type of intelligence in the form of good grades and academic achievements.

- **Practical intelligence:** This type of intelligence is characterized by problem-solving based on past experience. This can be as simple as knowing which street is unsafe to walk down, which step to skip, or which milk brand keeps the longest in the refrigerator.
- **Creative intelligence:** This type of intelligence is characterized by finding creative, or out-of-the-box, solutions to problems they experience. This could be in the form of solving plot holes in a story or fixing that leaky tap upstairs without calling a plumber.

Now, if you ask me, there is one more main type of intelligence. Can you guess what it is?

WHAT IS EMOTIONAL INTELLIGENCE?

Larger-than-life concepts like emotion and intelligence could really have entire books dedicated to exploring them in full—and they do. So, I'm sure you can imagine that emotional intelligence is no different. Luckily for you, I have this entire book to convey the full message of just how important and complex emotional intelligence can be.

If you missed it, I tried to cover the definition of emotional intelligence in just one sentence in the introduction. Emotional intelligence can be defined as the ability to identify, comprehend, and manage or influence one's own emotions and the emotions of others. That definition holds the key components that make up emotional intelligence.

- **Identifying emotions:** Some people can do this on "vibes" alone. Others need to read facial expressions and body language. This is the most basic level of emotional intelligence. It is simply the ability to identify not only how people around you are feeling but also how *you* are feeling.

- **Comprehending emotions:** Once you've identified how someone is feeling, the next step is making an educated guess as to *why* they are feeling that way. The goal is not always to get an exact answer, however. Sometimes, it is as simple as knowing that your partner isn't angry at something *you've* done, but rather that they are irritable after a long day at work.

- **Managing emotions:** This component is especially helpful in the aspect of self-control. Being able to regulate your own emotions is a skill that will work to your advantage a thousand times over—think stress and anger management. The other side of this component is managing the emotions of those around you. This may include being able to settle a rowdy group, cheer up a friend, or inspire action in teammates.

- **Leveraging emotions:** All the preceding components lend to this final one—being able to make decisions based on the information we've received. For example: You've discovered that your partner is upset and determined that it is, in fact, something that you've done. Now, instead of ignoring the problem as they're-in-a-bad-mood matter, you can react accordingly by apologizing and making up for your transgression. Emotional intelligence includes using emotions to promote positive thinking, creative problem-solving, and appropriate responses.

ASSESS YOUR OWN EMOTIONAL INTELLIGENCE

Now, much like IQ, your EI can be measured. There are two main tests that are used for scoring emotional intelligence. They are:

- The Mayer-Salovey-Caruso Emotional Intelligence Test (MSCEIT): Developed by doctors Mayer, Salovey, and Caruso, the MSCEIT is a series of objective and impersonal questions that test the respondent's ability to identify, comprehend, manage, and leverage emotions. Ideally, this assessment is completed in an environment where the respondent's performance can be observed by a professional, rather than relying on the respondent's personal assessment of their performance.
- The Emotional and Social Competence Inventory (ESCI): Developed by the Hay Group, the ECSI measures your EI on 12 scales, namely:

  - emotional self-awareness
  - emotional self-control
  - adaptability
  - achievement orientation
  - positive outlook
  - empathy
  - organizational awareness
  - coach and mentor
  - Inspirational leadership
  - influence
  - conflict management
  - teamwork

Before we go on to the assessment in this book, I must first disclaim that this is not a professional assessment of your emotional intelligence. This test exists only to give you a general idea of your emotional intelligence level. To get the best idea of your EI score, I would recommend taking the following assessments online and comparing your all scores.

- Psychology Today's Emotional Intelligence Test (45 minutes and 146 questions—payment required for full results).
- IHHP's EQ Quiz (5 minutes and 13 questions).
- Verywell Mind's "How Emotionally Intelligent Are You?" Quiz (5 minutes and 10 questions).
- The Personality Lab's EQ Test (10 minutes and 40 questions—payment required for results).

Your Emotional Intelligence Assessment

1. Are you able to understand your own emotions?

A. I'm very aware of my emotions and how they can impact my behavior.
B. Sometimes I struggle to identify my emotions, and I'm not always sure why I make the decisions I make.
C. I have a lot of difficulty identifying my own emotions, and even if I can, I don't know the reason behind them.

2. How often do you reflect and analyze your strengths and weaknesses?

A. Every year, I reflect on my strengths and weaknesses so that I can use the coming year to improve on myself.

B. I sometimes think about the things I am good and bad at, but I rarely work to change them.

C. I think I did something like that in high school once.

3. How do you deal with stressful situations?

A. I am usually able to keep a calm head and think rationally toward a resolution.

B. I try my best, but sometimes I snap under the pressure.

C. I'm a wreck. I get overwhelmed quickly and find it hard to control my reactions.

4. Do you stick to your long-term goals even through difficult times?

A. Obstacles and setbacks don't deter me from my goals. I am determined and persistent.

B. I often find myself derailed when problems arise, but I'm always able to find my way back on track.

C. I usually give up on my long-term goals when they become too difficult to achieve.

5. Do you understand the emotions of those around you?

A. I can pick up on the emotions of those around me and am able to empathize with them.

B. I can recognize how people around me are feeling, but I don't always understand why they feel that way.

C. I am usually more focused on how I am feeling.

6. What level of comfort do you experience in social situations?

A. Very comfortable. I am able to adapt to various social settings.
B. I'm usually awkward in social settings.
C. I don't like social situations at all. I'm always uncomfortable.

7. Are you able to handle conflicts in your relationships?

A. Communication is the key to resolving conflict calmly.
B. I avoid conflict as much as I can. I find it difficult to keep the situation calm and respectful.
C. I am usually the one causing conflict, and I struggle to compromise on a solution.

8. Are you able to maintain long-term relationships?

A. Yes. I have many strong friendships, and I take care to keep my relationships strong.
B. I have a few good friends, but I am known to go AWOL for weeks at a time, especially when I am stressed.
C. No. My relationships always seem to end before they grow into something meaningful.

Your Emotional Intelligence Results

Tally up your results based on the point assignment below. The higher your point total, the higher your emotional intelligence, and vice versa. The highest score possible for this assessment is 24, and the lowest is eight.

A: 3 points
B: 2 points
C: 1 point

Please don't be discouraged if you receive a low score. Remember that acknowledging the problem is the first step in solving that problem. This is only your starting point. This is the "before" that comes prior to your self-improvement. I know you can do this.

THE REASONS YOU NEED EMOTIONAL INTELLIGENCE

The emotion that can break your heart is sometimes the very one that heàls it.

— NICHOLAS SPARKS

When I sit and think about how I might convey the absolute complexity and cruciality of emotions to you, I come up short of words. However, I will try my best.

Researchers found that individuals between the ages of 17 and 60 interact with an average of 18–23 people every day (Del Valle et al., 2007). Every one of those interactions happens with an individual who has complex emotions—emotions that drive and influence their every move and decision. The same goes for you. Moreover, every time you interact with someone, your emotions influence theirs. Then they go on to interact with someone else, and the cycle continues.

A friendly and joyful word to someone having a bad morning may change the course of the rest of their day. Similarly, a rude and disinterested response may ruin someone's day and affect the rest of their interactions.

This is why emotional intelligence is such an important skill to possess. It doesn't only change the way you view and manage your own emotions; it also deeply affects those around you and, to an extent, the world around you.

STORIES TO INSPIRE

In case my words haven't yet convinced you of the importance of emotional intelligence, here are a few testimonies as to how EI can work to everyone's advantage.

A personal anecdote:

I once worked with a teacher who thrived off of taking credit for other teachers' ideas, work, and accomplishments. He was known for overselling how good he was at his job. After one of these occasions, where he had been bragging about his evaluation score, he left some papers next to the copier. These papers happened to be his actual evaluation score—which was significantly less magnificent than he had sold it to be—and happened to be found by a colleague and me. This seemed like the perfect opportunity to expose him. She and I started planning how we would tell everyone after school and even laughed about certain colleagues who would get a kick out of this news. As we were talking, he walked into the copy room, looking distraught. He was unusually quiet as he took his papers and left the room. My colleague continued to revel in his eventual exposure. I stopped her and said that something seemed off with him, something more than just a bad evaluation. We decided against exposing him and later found out that his wife had left him completely out of the blue. At that moment, I read his emotions and immediately knew that I had to regulate my own emotions and behavior for the sake of a colleague, despite any previous frustrations.

Bradley from Utah, USA writes:

The morning of an important interview, I sat with my sister at the kitchen table. The anxiety must have been obvious to her because she suddenly turned to me, took my hand, and said; "You're incredibly capable. I know you want this, and you're going to get it. The only way you can fail yourself is by not showing up." I just stared at her in shock, but her words genuinely gave me the confidence I needed to put my best foot forward when I knew that otherwise, I would have just shown up out of obligation.

Milly from Ontario, Canada writes:

I was once at a Rock concert with a lot of people. One thing to understand is that, in a crowd like that, one punch could turn into an absolute brawl. Two guys behind me were getting into an argument because one of them was crushing the other's girlfriend in the crowd. Instead of minding my own business, I turned around and said, "There's space next to me." The girlfriend moved to stand beside me and in front of her boyfriend. Thankfully, no fights broke out that day.

TRAITS OF EMOTIONALLY INTELLIGENT PEOPLE

Now that you know your EI starting point and how much of an impact it can have, let us discuss the traits of someone with high emotional intelligence. There are a few reasons why recognizing the traits of an emotionally intelligent person may be useful.

Firstly, it lets you know who you can trust with your emotions. If you feel you need to talk to someone or even look up to someone as an example of what you'd like to be, then being able to recognize someone with these traits will prove beneficial.

Secondly, these traits can act as goals.

If you scored high in the emotional intelligence assessment, go through these traits and circle the ones you think you embody. The ones that aren't circled may be points of weakness for you. I've always said that weaknesses are just strengths that haven't hit the gym yet. These are areas where you can improve and grow even more emotionally intelligent.

If you scored low in the emotional intelligence assessment, go through these traits and circle the ones that you long to embody. Keep those traits at the forefront of your mind in every interaction, and do your best to practice them and accept them as part of your being (more on that in a future chapter).

Now, let us have a look at the four main traits of an emotionally intelligent individual.

Self-awareness

- This is the ability to identify, describe, and understand one's own emotions and how they are affecting your actions.
- Emotional self-awareness involves

  - knowing your strengths and weaknesses.
  - knowing when you are capable and when to rely on someone else's capabilities.
  - knowing your core values.

Self-management

- This is the ability to regulate one's own emotions, especially negative, disruptive, or impulsive emotions. Self-management traits include

  o Emotional self-control: the ability to remain calm in times of anxiety or anger.
  o Adaptability: the ability to accept and adapt to change.
  o Achievement orientation: the ability to accept feedback and improve performance.
  o Positive outlook: the ability to recognize opportunities and the good in people and situations. The ability to move on from mistakes.

Social awareness

- This is the ability to recognize and interpret the emotions of those around oneself and to read and respond to social cues. Social awareness traits include

  o Empathy: the ability to show genuine curiosity and care for those around you. This involves making an effort to fully understand how someone is feeling.
  o Organizational awareness: the ability to strategically coordinate people according to their emotions and their dynamics with others.

Relationship management

- This is the ability to interact with others in a meaningful way and to maintain important relationships. Relationship management traits include

  ○ Influence: the ability to motivate others and gain support for one's vision.
  ○ Coach and mentor: the ability to give productive and encouraging feedback.
  ○ Conflict management: the ability to settle disputes in a manner that benefits all.
  ○ Teamwork: the ability to work well with others, actively participate, take accountability, and share in success.
  ○ Inspirational leadership: the ability to inspire and lead others toward a certain goal.

PRACTICAL EXAMPLES OF EMOTIONAL INTELLIGENCE

Now we know what defines an emotionally intelligent person, but these things aren't always obvious to spot in someone. How are you supposed to know if Susan from accounting is practicing self-management or if she is just a calm and unbothered person? Here are some examples of behavior you might see in an emotionally intelligent person.

Emotionally intelligent people in

- the workplace are likely to

  ○ express their thoughts and ideas confidently and respectfully.

○ be compassionate with those who need them.
○ be flexible and resilient in the face of changes and challenges.
○ listen actively in and out of meetings.
○ be willing and eager to spend time together outside of work.
○ freely and consistently celebrate creativity and innovation.

- leadership positions are likely to

○ ensure a collective understanding of goals.
○ create a strategic plan to achieve the goals and assign tasks to those with the strengths needed to complete them.
○ design and maintain a strong vision and identity for their team.
○ establish an appreciation and knowledge of how important work activities and behaviors are.
○ show appreciation and recognition for contributions.
○ embrace changes and encourage flexibility.
○ foster trust, enthusiasm, confidence, optimism, and cooperation.

- a learning environment are likely to

○ listen to understand.
○ include others.
○ share with others.
○ let others know they are needed.
○ take turns.
○ encourage others.
○ compromise to settle disputes.
○ volunteer to do their part.

- a relationship are likely to

  - remain calm, even when they don't get what they want.
  - have their own friends outside of the relationship.
  - have their own boundaries and respect yours.
  - not take out their temper on you if they're having a bad day.
  - talk to you if they are unhappy about something.
  - want to know everything about you.

- a family unit are likely to

  - take care of themselves as well as others.
  - be generous in expressing their love and appreciation.
  - listen and communicate well with you.
  - tend to each person's individual needs as well as the whole family unit's needs.
  - teach and model emotionally intelligent traits.
  - take responsibility for their mistakes.
  - not immediately jump into problem-solving mode before tending to emotional needs.

NEED FOR EMOTIONAL INTELLIGENCE

Okay, so emotional intelligence is important. Hopefully, that's come across by now. However, you may still be wondering what the relevance is. Why is EI needed? Will it change every area of my life? Let's take the workplace as an example: Will emotional intelligence really help me reach my goals?

I feel like you may know my answer: Yes! Emotional intelligence plays a significant role in helping businesses and individuals adapt to ever-changing environments and markets. Emotional intelligence has a profound impact on organizational learning, decision-making, and leadership.

- **Organizational learning** refers to on-the-job learning that must take place for a business to keep up with market, technology, and political changes. Think of how many new systems were put into place during the COVID-19 pandemic or how often technology changes the way a certain job can be done. If employees are able to adapt well to change and remain calm in stressful situations, these transitions are made much smoother, more effective, and more successful, and—speaking from experience—it helps everyone keep their sanity!
- **Decision-making** has the ability to render us catatonic. Some of us become paralyzed by the overwhelming emotion behind each decision. Some of us react impulsively without considering all the options. However, an emotionally intelligent person has the ability to remain level-headed no matter the overwhelm. Imagine how many businesses closed preemptively because their CEOs could not decide on a strategy to keep the business going.
- **Leadership** requires organizational learning and decision-making skills. So, we can already count +2 points for EI right there. We must also remember that everything in a business is reliant on good leadership. An inspiring and motivational leader can truly save a business from going under. A leader who has high EI is sure to cultivate a workplace environment based on EI. This ensures that each employee under that leader is sure to be skilled in organizational learning and decision-making as well.

IMPACT OF EMOTIONAL INTELLIGENCE...

Okay, so EI is beneficial to others and to your workplace, but what about you? But what do you get out of putting in the time and effort to improve your EI? Don't worry. I won't say," You'll get bragging rights!" or, "You'll get the peace of mind that comes with knowing you're helping those around you." No. I'm here to tell you that improving your emotional intelligence holds as many advantages for you as an individual as it does for those around you.

... on Your Health

First, and you may not initially believe me on this one, emotional intelligence has a positive impact on your physical and mental health. But it's proven. A study conducted by Fernández-Abascal and Martín-Díaz in 2015 found that high emotional intelligence related to

- an increase in

  - wellness maintenance
  - enhancement behaviors
  - accident control behaviors

- and a decrease in

  - traffic risk-taking
  - substance risk-taking
  - risk-taking behaviors

This study is proof that an improved EI leads to a healthier lifestyle. Those with high EI are less likely to take unnecessary risks and more inclined to prioritize wellness, accident control, and self-improvement. So, emotional intelligence makes you better at making yourself better.

Furthermore, the emotional regulation that comes with a high EI is linked to better heart health. A high EI also improves one's ability to keep up with a treatment plan and lifestyle changes, such as the kind that comes with type 2 diabetes, i.e., blood sugar control.

That's not all, though. Many other studies have been done that prove EI's impact on your mental health. Many of these studies are cited in a paper by Farrahi et al. (2015). They found that higher EI leads to

- lower physiological distress
- lower levels of anxiety
- lower levels of depression
- lower levels of anger, shame, jealousy, fear, and sadness

... at the Workplace

Next, the workplace. And let's be honest, anything that makes life at work better is heaven-sent. For the majority, most of our time is spent at work. And I don't know about you, but even when I am not at work, I am thinking about work. So, I could really benefit from anything that could make my work life more enjoyable.

And, you guessed it: EI does just that.

As we get through the chapters in this book, you will learn how intricately each of these aspects is bolstered and boosted by improving your EI:

- engagement
- productivity
- attention capacity
- adaptability
- motivation
- creativity
- effectiveness
- performance

Beyond just these aspects, though, emotional intelligence's largest impact is usually on the self and our interpersonal relationships. When we're able to maintain healthier relationships in the workplace, it improves our overall working experience. Everyone works as a team toward a common goal. Everyone communicates. Everyone cares deeply about the work and about each other.

And, if we combine the improved working aspects and the improved relationships with colleagues—and even superiors—our opportunities for promotions and career progression are increased as well. Suddenly, our success becomes more tangible—our goals start getting closer than they were before, more attainable.

... on Your Quality of Life

The influence of emotional intelligence within professional settings serves as a gateway to recognizing its incredible effects on enhancing the overall quality of life. The impact of emotional intelligence leads to greater satisfaction in both personal and professional realms and ultimately fosters a deeper sense of happiness and fulfillment. This is how:

- **Personal satisfaction**: A study conducted by Divya Rahul Jain in 2015 showed that there is a positive relationship between life satisfaction and emotional intelligence—although the report only marks this relationship in females. This study found that when women multi-tasked, they became stressed, and their quality of life decreased. However, with higher EI, women were less likely to multi-task and, thus, were less stressed and found more satisfaction in life.
- **Professional satisfaction**: A study conducted by Suleman et al. in 2020 says, "Emotional intelligence is a basic variable that ensures the job satisfaction of individuals and hence stimulates the overall productivity of an organization." A positive correlation was discovered between job satisfaction and emotional intelligence across five dimensions: altruism, relationship management, integrity, emotional stability, and self-development.
- **Happiness**: When you are able to maintain more fulfilling relationships and are more adept at managing stressful situations, you become a happier and more positive person.

... on Your Relationships

Beyond personal, professional, and life satisfaction, emotional intelligence plays a massive role in relationships. Now, when I say "relationship," most people think of romantic relationships. However, there are many other interpersonal relationships in one's life, such as familial relationships, work relationships, or simple friendships. A higher EI is the key to maintaining these relationships. The main reason for this is that we are able to perceive the changes that occur in ourselves and others. When we are sensitive to the change in dynamics, we are able to adjust accordingly.

There are eight areas in which EI improves personal relationships.

- starting with a good core friendship
- mutual and genuine respect
- practicing healthy boundaries
- effective communication
- noticing and supporting what is meaningful to the other
- conflict management
- living life together
- encouraging the relationship

But not all relationships are personal. Emotional intelligence can also help improve many of our business relationships. Improved relationships in the workplace make work life easier, but improved customer relationships are another way in which EI can help our professional careers soar. Imagine being your client's favorite person to deal with. Whenever they need something, you're the first one they call. In customer relations, EI helps us to:

- remember the client's personal details that allow us to acknowledge them as more than a client—a friend.
- explore shared interests and experiences to build rapport.
- use more informal language without professional jargon that makes the customer feel more comfortable.
- admit our faults and mistakes, and remind our clients that we are people, too.

... at Home

If we're not at work, we're at home. And, unfortunately, it's not always the healthiest environment. But if we can improve our work life with emotional intelligence, we can surely improve our home life as well. And it comes back to our interpersonal relationships with those we love most.

Improving our awareness and empathy is the first step toward abolishing misunderstandings and miscommunications that can tear a family apart from the inside. Improved EI helps us recognize when our family members need help, and it helps us respond to those needs appropriately.

Furthermore, when we know ourselves inside and outside, we are shielded against manipulation. We are acutely aware of when we are at fault and can take accountability rather than assigning blame to the first person we see.

The most impactful way that EI can improve our family life is by improving our communication skills.

THE DARK SIDE OF EMOTIONAL INTELLIGENCE

I've gone on for quite a while about how great and good and important emotional intelligence is. However, I am not naive. I know that emotional intelligence, like most things, can be used malevolently. There are people in the world who can use good tools for bad purposes. Managing emotions—in the wrong hands—can transform into manipulating emotions. Regulating emotions can transform into disguising emotions.

While exploring the dark side of emotional intelligence, the awestruck (or dumbstruck) effect was found. This is the effect that an emotionally intelligent speaker can have on their audience. This effect left the listeners less likely to criticize the message. Listeners also claim to remember more of the message while actually recalling less of it. Now, imagine an emotionally intelligent speaker convincing a crowd of awful things. Listeners are moved by this message, less likely to criticize it, and—even though they may forget most of the message—are still willing to act on it.

BECOMING AN EMOTIONAL SCIENTIST

Okay, the introductory class is now over. This is where the real learning begins—where notes and actions must be taken. And our first lesson starts right back at the beginning: emotions. Learning how to read your own emotions and the emotions of others is the first, most basic, and perhaps most useful skill in this book.

Emotions have three main functions. They

- tell us when something in our life is changing or needs attention.
- drive our every action and decision.
- alert others when we're dealing with stress or sadness and may need support.

This is true for ourselves and for everyone whose emotions we may be attempting to read. However, the way we choose to interpret and understand those emotions plays a big role in determining how useful that information could be.

EMOTIONAL SCIENTIST VS. EMOTIONAL JUDGE

There are two main ways in which you can interpret emotions. Depending on which way you choose to do so, you can be identified as either an emotional judge or an emotional scientist.

An emotional judge is critical and impulsive. Emotional judges don't care to know or understand how others are feeling. They are quick to assume how someone is feeling, even so far as to tell others how they should be feeling.

Emotional scientists, on the other hand, love to learn more about emotions—their own and others. They are curious and analytical. They want to know and understand how others are feeling. Just like any good scientist, they will listen actively, investigate, and come up with theories about the emotions of others. They also spend significant time trying to understand and manage their own emotions.

The first step toward improving your emotional intelligence is abandoning the emotional judge mentality and embracing the habits of an emotional scientist.

STEP 1: IMPROVE EMOTIONAL LITERACY

We've spoken a lot about being able to identify and name emotions in oneself and in others. This ability is emotional literacy. Emotional literacy also involves the appropriate expression of emotion. Psychotherapist Claude Steiner (1979), the one who is thought to have coined the term, introduced emotional literacy as having five components:

- empathy
- knowing one's feelings
- managing one's emotions
- emotional interactivity
- repairing emotional problems

The tool we use to remain in control of our emotions is called emotional literacy. If we have sufficient emotional literacy, it prevents us from being confused, overwhelmed, impulsive, and overrun by our emotions. It helps us to "read the room" and react accordingly to other people's emotions.

Although we are born with emotions, emotional literacy is something that must be developed over time. It doesn't matter at what point you're starting or at what stage of life; there is always room for improvement. And you can start right now and practice every day. It's super easy.

Learn to name your emotions.

STEP 2: IMPROVE EMOTIONAL VOCABULARY

Kircanski et al. conducted a study in 2012, testing the power of naming your emotions. Participants were asked to stand 5 ft away from a tarantula and then step incrementally closer to the tarantula until they were to touch the tarantula. For some participants, this was all they were asked to do. But some were told to name how they felt after each step toward the spider. When the researchers studied the results, they found that the group that labeled their emotions had lower physiological reactivity to the spider. In fact, the participants who spoke aloud more fear or anxiety words had even lower reactivity.

Here's how I like to think of it: Imagine your emotion as a Karen. For those of you who don't know, a "Karen" is an entitled person who is typically female, typically Caucasian, and typically loud, obnoxious, and sticks their noses where they don't belong.

Imagine you're in a confrontation with this Karen, and they say, "Do you know who I am?" Your heart drops. You don't know who they are. They very well could be someone with power, influence, and authority who could make your life hell.

Except your friend stands up (in this analogy, your friend is your EI), points this Karen down, and says, "I do know who you are! You're Karen from down the road and you don't run me.

All of a sudden, that terror vanishes, and your confidence returns. You have no reason to fear this person. You know who they are, and you know that they have no power over you.

Emotions are the same way. You name them, and they lose their hold over you. This doesn't mean you can't or shouldn't feel those emotions. It simply means that they cannot control you.

But that might be easier said than done for some. If that's true for you, try the following steps in the coming days:

Step 1: Take note of when your emotions change. At this point, you don't yet have to make note of why your emotions changed, only that they did.

Step 2: Take note of how your body is feeling. Any telltale signs that hint toward how you're feeling?

Step 3: Take note of what you're thinking. What is your inner monologue like, positive or negative?

Step 4: Try to name your emotions. Be as accurate as you can.

And if you are still a little in the dark about what name matches the feeling, here are some resources to familiarize yourself with the appropriate vocabulary:

- Verywell Family's "List of "Feeling Words from A to Z"
- Karla McLaren's "Your Emotional Vocabulary List"
- The Conflict Center's "Expanding Your Emotional Vocabulary"

STEP 3: UNDERSTAND THAT EMOTIONS ARE DATA

For many people, emotions act as instructions. When you feel something, you act on it without question. However, emotions are not instructions. They are information. They are data. Thinking this way can change the way you approach and engage with your emotions and the emotions of others. It can help us make informed guesses and decisions.

But let's not forget that we're talking about emotions here. And, just like data, they are variable—they change, and they change quickly! And, because emotions can change so quickly, it would be foolish to think they can define someone's character or abilities. For example, if someone becomes agitated in a tough situation, it does not mean they're an incapable or negative person.

How does looking at emotions as data change the way we approach emotions?

- **A strategical approach**

Because our emotions are information and not instructions, we can make our own logical decisions about whether or not following our emotions will take us where we want to go. It helps us regulate our emotions because we can assess how the emotion can aid or hinder our actions.

- **Assisting with sympathy**

Understanding emotions, especially from another person's point of view, can seem like a gargantuan task. However, understanding the information might be a bit easier. You may find it easier to recognize that actions that may have felt like personal attacks were only emotional reactions. You may find it easier to recognize that someone is too deeply connected to a topic to *want* to understand a different opinion. This can help you approach and react more appropriately. For example: During a heated debate about which route would be best to take during their road trip, Alex can't help but feel like Sarah is judging his navigation skills. He'd be the one driving, after all. So he should be the one making that decision. But suddenly, Alex realizes that Sarah's mood has shifted. She's not just arguing anymore. She's upset—her cheeks are red and she's avoiding eye contact. He doesn't understand why, but he recognizes that Sarah is really passionate about taking this other route. So, he changes his approach and asks if there is something on the other route she'd like to do or if there's something that bugs her about the route he'd like to take. She responds and says that his route takes them through a dangerous part of town where a friend of hers was attacked. She wouldn't feel safe there and feels like Alex doesn't care about that. Suddenly, everything makes sense. Alex assures

Sarah that he does care about her safety and that he would never let anything happen to her, but if she really wants to take the other route and be safer, he'd be happy to do so.

- **Addressing the source**

Information, much like an emotion, doesn't come out of nowhere. There is always a source, an underlying reference. Just like any good scientist, we must take the time to check out and try to understand the source. Doing this helps us understand the information—the emotion—much better and what to do with it.

STEP 4: LEARNING TO IDENTIFY EMOTIONAL TRIGGERS

In Chapter 1, we spoke about how important identifying emotional triggers is. Identifying our triggers and understanding them gives us the insight we need to deal with the emotions that are triggered. However, identifying our emotional triggers takes practice. Your body usually prioritizes the emotion that was triggered. So, redirecting your attention is a conscious effort. Here are a few steps to take if you're struggling:

- **Step 1:** Identify when you have been triggered. Listen to your body—it will let you know. When your heart starts pounding or your stomach turns, don't ignore it. Take note of it and start making connections to how different emotions make your body react. These strong physical reactions are our biggest hint that something has affected us.
- **Step 2:** Take a moment. Acknowledge the emotion, but

allow yourself the time to first process the triggering event. Give yourself permission.

- **Step 3:** Identify the event. What happened that could have initiated this response? It may be obvious, but more likely, you will have to put in effort to identify why you started feeling this way.
- **Step 4:** Flashback time. Consider what other events in your life have made you feel this way. Consider—if you are able to—what was the first event ever to make you feel this way? What is the origin of this trigger?
- **Step 5:** Approach with compassion. Don't see these triggers as negative. Instead, approach them with curiosity. Remember that getting to know your emotions better is an advantage. Deal with the situation and emotions with compassion for yourself and for whoever was involved.

This is the "Stop, Drop, and Roll" method. Steps 1 and 2 are when you "stop." You take a moment. You acknowledge the changes, and you make the decision to address them. Steps 3 and 4 are when you "drop" yourself into the emotion and into the event to truly analyze it. This step is when you take control of your emotions rather than letting them become you.

Finally, you "roll." You respond, and you proceed after having identified the trigger. But how does one "roll" after having been triggered?

- Breathe.
- Ground yourself. Use your five senses to ground yourself and not be taken away by your emotions. Name

- o 5 things that you can see.
- o 4 things that you can touch.
- o 3 things that you can hear.
- o 2 things that you can smell.
- o 1 thing that you can taste.

- Talk to someone. Discuss the trigger and the emotions with someone you trust.
- Take care of yourself. Take a walk or a hot bath to soothe yourself.
- Journal the experience, the thoughts, and the emotions. Write down what you learned. Get it off your chest.
- Choose a coping statement for these moments, and practice repeating that coping statement.

THREADING BODY, MIND, AND HEART

You'll remember that in the description of what an emotion is, there are three main components: physiological, behavioral, and subjective. In other words, body, mind, and heart. Emotions affect us on these three levels, and therefore, managing emotions requires addressing all three of these levels. However, the heart and mind often overwhelm the senses. Sure, you can feel your stomach turning, but the more concerning bit is the sense of dread and terror in your heart.

Ignoring the body means that there is an entire level that is going unaddressed. To fully manage our emotions, that level must be considered.

One way to do this is to perform a full body scan. This allows you to focus on the physiological reactions rather than what the heart and mind are doing. This will improve your self-awareness and self-control. Performing a full body scan can be a short activity or a full meditation. It begins at the crown of your head and slowly moves down your body. Be sure to spend at least a minute on each part of your body and give your full attention to each sensation you feel.

GENERATING AWARENESS ABOUT YOURSELF

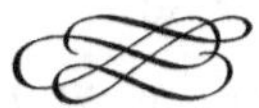

There is no self development without self-awareness. You can read as many books as you like, but if you're unable to read yourself you'll never learn a thing.

— STEVEN BARTLETT

Do you think you would have ever picked up this book without realizing you needed to improve your emotional intelligence? Maybe you didn't pick up this book. Maybe it was given to you by a caring friend. This is the chapter where you figure out why.

I know it sounds cheesy, but there is truly only one person who spends your entire lifetime with you, and it's you. There is a reason why self-love, self-care, and even self-awareness are so important. Nobody wants a toxic relationship, even with themselves.

But there's something many people don't realize about toxic relationships. And it's that they can go unnoticed for so long because those experiencing them simply don't realize it. It's time to realize! It's time to do a compatibility test with yourself! It's only right that you get to know the person you'll be spending the rest of your life with.

WHAT IS SELF-AWARENESS?

Self-awareness is a goal. True self-awareness is not really a thing you do so much as it is something you are. Much like many of the topics discussed in this book, self-awareness is a process. You can start anywhere and grow from there.

Self-awareness starts developing during infancy and continues as you grow, usually following this process.

Differentiation: acknowledging one's own reflection.

Situation: recognizing one's own reflection and recognizing one's own movements as one's own.

Identification: knowing one's reflection actually belongs to oneself, or looking in the mirror and saying, "That is me."

Permanence: recognizing oneself in images, even if one's appearance has changed.

Self-consciousness: becoming aware of oneself from the perspective of others, or becoming aware that other people have different perceptions of you.

I am sure that everyone reading has a basic understanding of what self-awareness is: the knowledge and comprehension of our passions, values, goals, behavior, thoughts, feelings, strengths, weaknesses, and our impact on others. In other words, self-awareness is knowing who we are, down to our cores.

But did you know that is only part of self-awareness—or rather, it's only one type of awareness? This type of self-awareness is private or internal self-awareness.

The second type of self-awareness is public or external. It involves knowing and understanding how the people around us perceive us according to all those same factors. Yes, knowing how other people see you is part of self-awareness.

I remember the moment I realized I needed to prioritize self-awareness. I was having a conversation with a friend who was sharing good news with me. Her good news resonated with me and excited me. So, I interrupted her and asked a question to clarify what she'd said.

"I was about to tell you before you interrupted me," she laughed, continuing to finish her story. At that moment, I was reminded of a conversation with a sibling the night before, where I had said the exact same thing because it always frustrates me when people interrupt me.

It reminded me of a quote by Inyanla Vanzant (2017): "Everyone comes into our lives to mirror back to us some part of ourselves we cannot or will not see." That's when I knew I had to work on fixing the behavior in myself that bothered me.

CHARACTERISTICS OF PEOPLE WHO HAVE LOW SELF-AWARENESS

At this point, you may be thinking, "Well, I know myself pretty well. In fact, I even know how others see me. So, I guess I am two for two!" That's great. However, I know there are going to be some of you who are panicking. Not because you don't think you're self-aware, but because you don't know whether or not you're self-aware. I didn't know for sure when I started my journey. It's not always easy to tell.

Yes, self-awareness is our second big step toward improving emotional intelligence. But emotional intelligence is like a relay race. Once you complete the first sprint, you hand over the baton, and the next one begins. So, think of this as the starting point of the next section of the EI race!

Let's look at a few characteristics of someone with a lack of self-awareness. While looking at these characteristics, I'm going to ask you to do something difficult. But it's important to remember that we can't fix what we don't acknowledge. I want you to circle the characteristics that apply to you. Try to be as honest as you can with yourself. This is just between you and this book. And, unlike in previous chapters, this time, circled traits are the things we want to minimize and unlearn.

- You believe you're at the top of your game. You've reached every goal and earned every success.
- You have trouble admitting when you've made a mistake. Okay, you would never admit to making a mistake.
- You don't take criticism well, and you often feel victimized.
- You openly criticize others. (No, constructive and helpful criticism doesn't count.)
- Everyone seems to cause drama with you, or there's always drama around you.
- You tend to avoid making tough decisions at all costs.
- But once your mind is made up, no one will convince you otherwise.
- The words "I don't know" don't exist in your vocabulary.

- When someone asks how you're really doing, you give vague responses.
- You need to be in control of everything.
- You're constantly worrying about the future and/or the past.
- You're a chatterbox, and what you say is often negative, or it's gossip.
- You value short-term happiness over long-term wellness.

HOW SELF-AWARE PEOPLE LOOK AND BEHAVE

Think about how many people know the real you. How many people have you let past all the guards you've put in place? It's in our nature to put up emotional shields and defense mechanisms to protect ourselves. The problem is that those defense mechanisms often turn into unhelpful behaviors such as denial, overthinking, and recurring patterns of guilt, self-hatred, and sadness.

These are the habits of those who aren't self-aware. You'll notice that those who have self-awareness lead a more peaceful and happier life. Why? Because self-awareness promotes healthier behaviors and habits. These positive habits are how you can identify someone with self-awareness. They're also habits you can start adding to your own daily life to improve and practice self-awareness.

- They're good listeners. They listen more than they speak, and they listen with curiosity and enthusiasm. They practice active listening, which is a concept we will get into later in the book.
- They appreciate feedback and take any opportunity to grow

and improve themselves. They'll often ask for constructive criticism, and they take feedback very well.

- They love learning more about themselves. They're curious about how their mind works, why they feel certain things, their strengths and weaknesses, and their emotional triggers. They want to know these things.
- They think about themselves. They are introspective and consider their thoughts, feelings, and behavior. It doesn't help you notice things about yourself if you immediately forget them.

HOW TO BE MORE SELF-AWARE

Those habits I mentioned before are habits you can build up to. Those are the habits of someone who is already self-aware. Here are a few habits for those of you who are at the beginning of your self-awareness journey.

- Learn from other people's mistakes. When you notice someone doing something that bothers you, ask yourself why it bothers you. Is it a reflection on something you do or something about yourself that you're unhappy with?
- Start asking for feedback. Learn what your weaknesses are and embrace them. Remember to take this criticism well. This is a learning experience.
- Recognize cognitive distortions that may alter your thoughts and beliefs. The human mind works in mysterious ways, and sometimes we can believe something wholly untrue just because of the way it was taught to us and how our subconscious has processed it. Take note of when these distortions influence your thoughts, beliefs, and feelings.

- Practice observing your thoughts without strings attached. Don't attach beliefs or emotions to your thoughts, and re-evaluate if you still align yourself with those thoughts. Remember that you are not your thoughts.

But don't worry; I'm human too, and I have been through this process. I know that learning new habits is easier said than done, especially intangible habits like these. So, here are a few practical things you can do to get started on your self-awareness journey:

- Identify and expose yourself to your emotional kryptonite. Learning to tolerate the worst feeling you can think of will help you gain a lot of insight into yourself.
- Reading high-quality fiction can teach us a lot about how to be more observant, how to be compassionate, and how emotions guide people toward certain decisions.
- Learn a new skill. This is an amazing way to foster a feeling of flexibility and newness that can aid in your journey to look deeper into yourself with new, fresh eyes.
- Draw a timeline of your life and evaluate how you feel about things that happened in the past versus how you felt while living through them. Consider how this changes your view of your current situation.

SELF-AWARENESS QUESTIONS

The following questions are guides for introspection and reflection. They're meant to encourage you to really take a good look at yourself. Use these as journaling opportunities and be as honest as possible. Remember that changing and improving your life can only work if you acknowledge the truth. While answering these questions, take note of any significant emotions that arise.

Questions About Your Personality

1. How would you describe yourself in three words?
2. How do you think your friends would describe you in three words?
3. What are your favorite qualities about yourself?
4. Has your personality changed since childhood? How so?
5. Is your personality similar to your parents' personalities? How so?
6. What are some of your fears?
7. Are you a logical or intuitive person?
8. What are your strengths?
9. What are your weaknesses?

Questions About Your Values and Goals

1. What does the perfect you look like?
2. Make a list of the most important things in your life. There are no rules for this. If it's important to you, write it down.
3. Now, next to each of those things, write down how much time you dedicate to them.
4. What are your dreams and goals?
5. Why are these your dreams and goals?
6. What is keeping you from achieving these dreams and goals?

Questions About Your Relationships

1. What does your perfect relationship look like?
2. Who is the person you have loved the most? Why?
3. Describe the best moment you've had in a relationship. Why is it the best one?

4. Now describe the worst moment. Why was it the worst?

5. How satisfied are you in your current relationship?

6. If a loved one called and said they only had a few more minutes to live, what would you say to them?

7. Do you treat yourself better than you treat others?

SELF-AWARENESS ACTIVITIES

In the pursuit of improved emotional intelligence, self-awareness stands as a cornerstone, fostering a deeper understanding of one's thoughts, emotions, and actions. Engaging in targeted self-awareness activities can serve as a powerful catalyst, lighting the way for transformative introspection and growth.

Grounding

Grounding is a great exercise in mindfulness—an exercise to refocus your attention on the present moment rather than getting lost in your emotions and thoughts. One of the best techniques to practice grounding is called the Grounding Chair.

1. Sit in a comfortable chair with your eyes closed and your feet firmly on the floor.

2. Spend some time to focus on your breathing. Take deep breaths, inhaling and exhaling on the count of three.

3. Bring your attention to your body—the way your back feels against the chair, the way your feet feel against the floor, or how your clothes feel against your skin.

4. Visualize grounding yourself—imagine pushing your feet down into the ground and letting the energy flow out of you and into the ground.

5. As you visualize the energy draining from you, let each body part go heavy and relax each muscle.

6. Feel all that heaviness fall out of your body and into the ground.

Developing Self-Acceptance/Examining Self-Measurement

Part 1:

Take two pieces of paper, marking one with "positive list" and the other with "negative list." Spend some time writing down both the positive and negative things you tell yourself. Focus on thoughts that make you feel either positive or negative. Evaluate the balance of positive versus negative statements. Are you particularly negative toward yourself? Do the negative statements seem as true and real now that they're written out?

Take the negative list, rip it into pieces, and throw it in the bin. Take the positive list and put it somewhere where you'll regularly see it.

Part 2:

Take another paper and make another list. Write down the following items on your list:

- height
- weight
- color of skin
- how we express our feelings
- the year we were born
- how we handle anxiety
- the size of our families
- the color of our eyes

Next to each of these items, make note of whether or not it is a part of yourself that you are in control of—in other words, that you are able to change. If you can think of any other things to list, write them down and make note of how many things are truly in your control.

If something is within your control and can be changed for the better, take note of it as a possible goal to work toward. You can even take it one step further by planning your first actionable steps toward achieving it.

If something is not within your control, note it as something to learn to accept about yourself.

NOT LIMITING YOURSELF

I have found in my own life that people can grow comfortable very quickly. Even when we're unhappy, even when we know we need to change, we don't want to. We're scared to change anything or do anything new because we've grown comfortable. I've also learned that nobody can grow in comfort. Why would we push ourselves if we're desperate to stay where we are, even if it's not where we want to be?

While researching for this book, I came across a Reddit post that really moved me. According to this Reddit poster (u/throw-away4rltnshp, 2021), there are three steps to manifesting the person you want to become.

1. Believe that you are already the person you want to be.
2. Believe that other people already see you as the person you want to be.
3. Take action to be the person you want to be—behave the way they would behave and believe the things they believe.

So, the next step in our journey is to push the boundaries. We need to leave our comfort zone because growth cannot happen if we're comfortable. That little voice telling us that we should stay put and live in this comfort—the one that says even if we try, we won't make it—we need to shut it up.

WHAT ARE SELF-LIMITING BELIEFS?

The main culprit as to why we choose to stay in our comfort zones is our self-limiting beliefs. Self-limiting beliefs are perceptions you have about yourself and the world that hold you back in some way. An important thing to remember about self-limiting beliefs is that they aren't just passing thoughts. They are firm beliefs that someone has, even if there may be evidence disputing those ideas.

Self-limiting beliefs are a negative side effect of ineffective self-awareness. They are the result of someone reflecting on themself and coming to an incorrect conclusion, or allowing what they learn about themself to become an excuse to stay in their comfort zone. Self-limiting beliefs can lead to depression, imposter syndrome, anxiety, and so on.

Self-limiting beliefs can also lead to self-limiting behaviors, such as

- Catastrophizing: assuming the worst will happen and using that as a reason to change your mind. The reasoning for this is usually to "protect" oneself, but often the worst-case scenario is very unlikely to happen.
- Labeling: assigning a label to ourselves when we are struggling because it is the label that has been put on others when they are struggling. For example, that person failed because they're stupid. Therefore, I failed because I am

stupid, not because of all the life events that have kept me from dedicating time to my studies.

- Fortune telling: Similar to catastrophizing, this is when we assume we know how something will play out and, therefore, we don't even try. The thought pattern is often, "What's the point if I know how it will end?"
- Taking responsibility: Unlike healthy accountability, this is when we hold ourselves responsible for every negative thing that happens around us, even if it is something completely out of our control.
- Mind Reading: assuming we know the reasons why other people do the things they do and projecting our assumptions onto the person. For example, when a friend cancels plans with you, you assume it must be because they've grown bored of the friendship and of you.

ARE YOU AWARE OF YOUR BELIEFS?

When self-limiting beliefs have been a part of someone's life for long enough, it's difficult to tell them apart from all the other beliefs. In fact, self-limiting beliefs can disguise themselves as knowing one's own strengths and weaknesses. However, self-awareness, such as knowing one's own weaknesses, is not the same as self-limiting beliefs.

Knowing our weaknesses gives us the opportunity to grow further. It helps us to re-evaluate where we should be pushing our time and efforts in a healthy way. Self-limiting beliefs are often false, and they always keep us stagnant.

However, the fact remains that they are beliefs. And similar to good and healthy beliefs, self-limiting beliefs are a part of us. They play a role in our decision-making, and we act on our beliefs subconsciously.

This is also known as operating on autopilot. Operating on autopilot is a behavior in which someone does not think through their decisions—they react impulsively. Sometimes, this can be a good thing. The "gut feeling" has laid claim to many successes over the years. However, autopilot decisions based on self-limiting beliefs are seldom positive.

Operating on self-limiting autopilot leads to negative behaviors that can influence not only us but also everyone we work with and interact with. It may lead to a defensive and, possibly, aggressive reaction to constructive criticism or a remark from a friend. It may lead to sarcastic remarks in inappropriate situations.

Self-limiting beliefs are more than just negative thought patterns. They can become ingrained in our very personalities, and that makes them extremely difficult to correct.

HOW ARE YOUR BELIEFS FORMED?

Like anything that is so ingrained in our personalities, self-limiting beliefs are formed at a young age and grow stronger over time. For instance, your parents may have had a negative experience with a policeman and regularly spoke about how much of a horrible person you must be to want to go into law enforcement like that. That might create a self-limiting belief within you. Regardless of your interests and desires, you would never consider going into law enforcement because a) you believe that everyone in law enforcement is horrible, and b) you believe that if you went into that career, your parents would think you're a horrible person. It may also guide you away from respecting police officers in the future.

However, it's often not as straightforward as that. Often, we form beliefs based on our experiences. So, we would get praised every time we brought home a good report card, but whenever we brought a piece of art home, we were told to focus on our studies. Over time, we come to believe that art is bad and studying is good. In fact, that may even lead to the belief that "I'm not good at art."

Furthermore, it is a tendency for the human mind to cling to an old belief, even when new information is gathered. You may grow up and experience a police officer going out of their way to protect you. But your belief that all cops are bad may be so ingrained that you write it off because the cop must have been on his best behavior only because he's got a body cam on.

As you can see from this example alone, strong self-limiting beliefs can keep us from growth and new experiences.

SELF-LIMITING BELIEFS THAT ARE HOLDING YOU BACK

Okay, so you may be getting a grasp on why self-limiting beliefs can be detrimental to personal growth and acceptance. But what do self-limiting beliefs even look like? Here are a few examples. Try to see if any of them sound familiar to you. Perhaps now is the time to recognize them for what they are.

- I'm too young or old for this position or to try this hobby.
- I don't have the skills for this position or to try this hobby.
- That is a position for someone more creative or intelligent than I am.
- I don't have time to invest in this hobby or in myself.
- This isn't a job for a woman or a man.
- I won't ever be successful in my industry.

- People in that industry are boring.
- I'll never be (blank) because (blank).
- That person has more (blank) than I do, so I won't ever be as good as them.
- You can't trust anyone.
- I don't have enough money to invest in this hobby or in myself.
- People in that industry are pretentious and arrogant.

HOW TO OVERCOME YOUR SELF-LIMITING BELIEFS

Now that we know just how much self-limiting beliefs can hold us back and, hopefully, how to identify some of our own self-limiting beliefs, it's time to learn how to nip those in the bud. Our aim in this book is to become more emotionally intelligent and emotional scientists. One way to do that is to ensure the information we have about ourselves and the world is correct, not beliefs that hold us back.

Here are seven steps to overcome your self-limiting beliefs. Pick one self-limiting belief and try each of these steps to overcome it. You don't have to correct every belief in one sitting. Take it slow.

- **Step 1:** Acknowledge this belief and how it has protected you up until now. Thank this belief for keeping you safeguarded, and accept the idea that you are ready to let go of this belief.
- **Step 2:** Ask yourself how this belief is serving you and write down all the answers: the ways it has helped you and all the ways it has held you back and worked against your growth and development.

- **Step 3:** Ask yourself what if you're wrong about this belief. Write down all the evidence you have that proves the belief is false. Be objective with this until the information can really set in, and you can see this belief for what it was: false.
- **Step 4:** Forgive yourself for believing this self-limiting belief. Forgive yourself and anyone else involved in creating, developing, and reinforcing this belief. Accept, again, the knowledge that you are now letting go of this belief.
- **Step 5:** Write down a few alternative beliefs that may be truer than this self-limiting belief. The goal is to write down new beliefs that can replace the self-limiting one—beliefs that are empowering and will serve you better. Use the evidence you collected in the previous step to create and bolster this belief.
- **Step 6:** Test if any of these alternative beliefs are true. Try living a day with this new belief at the forefront of your mind. For one day, pretend you really believe this new belief to be true and act in accordance. See how differently you feel about the new belief and your old belief after trying it out for a day.
- **Step 7:** Always challenge this self-limiting belief when it turns up. Put yourself in situations that discredit that belief. Talk out loud and discount that belief. Let your mind and body know that you don't believe it anymore. This might be a daily struggle, and a great way to practice this is to create a mantra or affirmation that you repeat to yourself when that belief feels too heavy or too true.

THE BELIEF-TO-RESULTS CYCLE

The reason self-limiting beliefs have such a hold on us is that there is a clear connection between beliefs and results. There is a cycle where beliefs lead to results, and, in turn, those results lead to confirming those beliefs or discounting them and creating new beliefs.

This cycle follows the following trail:

Belief> Thoughts > Feelings > Actions > Results, and then back to Beliefs.

Each step in this cycle is influenced by the previous step and influences the next. This also means that each step is an opportunity to change the next and/or previous step. Each and every step of this cycle is an opportunity for growth and development.

This is great news for you. This means that if you are struggling to change your beliefs directly, there are four other avenues you can take. You can change your thoughts, your feelings, and your actions, and through your actions, you can change the results. And the same can be said for every other point. If you want the results to change, change one of the others. If you want your feelings to change, change one of the others.

This cycle is the secret to a significant change in our lives, because struggling to change just one of these aspects doesn't mean we've failed. It just opens the opportunity to change one of the others instead. And we may have more success with that and, as a result, end up changing the thing we originally wanted to change anyway.

There's more than one way to grow!

ARIANA HUFFINGTON ON SELF-DOUBT

Ariana Huffington is the president and editor-in-chief of The Huffington Post and once said, in an interview with Fast Company in 2014, that the thing that holds her back most is the voice inside her own head. Huffington calls this voice her "obnoxious roommate." Huffington says that she wishes there was some way to record the things we tell ourselves so we could realize how awful we can be to ourselves and why it's imperative that we stop. Perhaps if we could hear how bad it actually is, we'd have a bigger urge to stop it (Giang, 2014).

The problem with these inner thoughts is that they are often reinforced by the outside world. Huffington mentions how news and information are often designed in a way to enhance the things our "obnoxious roommate" says about us. But it's important to push against the obnoxious roommate "with a dose of wisdom," says Huffington.

INVITING DISCUSSION OF EMOTIONAL INTELLIGENCE

"As much as 80% of adult "success" comes from EQ."

— DANIEL GOLEMAN

Emotional intelligence doesn't get enough of the limelight when we talk about communication, in my opinion. Most misunderstandings and miscommunications come from a failure to understand the emotions of someone else, and it's possible that the reason you came to be reading this book in the first place is because this is something you're familiar with.

Not being able to understand or empathize with the way someone else is feeling puts an immediate barrier between you, and if this is something that happens over and over again, it can become a problem for the relationship. Many people come away from this situation feeling like they're the problem and that they're inadequate or stupid in some way, when the reality is, that their emotional intelligence simply needs a little bit of training. Some people try to figure it out on their own, and others might look into improving their communication skills – but unless they improve their ability to read and empathize with other people's emotions, those skills will only get them so far. Emotional intelligence must also be part of the conversation.

It's with this in mind that I'm interrupting our flow a little here. Now that you're this far through the book, I'd like to ask for your help in bringing this to light. The more discussion there is about emotional intelligence and the ability we have to train ourselves in it, the fewer people will run into these problems. We can start by talking about the contents of this book and helping other people to find it. And that's where you come in! I'd like to ask you to take a few moments to leave your feedback online.

By leaving a review of this book, you'll keep the conversation about emotional intelligence alive and help other people to find the information that will help them.

Reviews don't just help to make sure that content stays visible and gets into the hands of the people who are looking for it; they allow us to keep discussions of important topics in the public sphere – and that's beneficial for everybody.

Thank you so much for your support. Knowledge is a powerful tool – especially when we share it.

THE MOTIVATING COMPONENT OF EMOTIONAL INTELLIGENCE

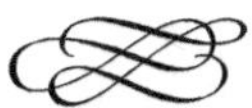

I used to be someone that struggled with motivation. We live in a world where everyone is expected to be motivated all the time, and even without motivation, they are expected to push through and achieve anyway. But working without motivation doesn't amount to anything good. The work will be passionless and done for the sake of getting it done. Furthermore, a lack of motivation leads to depression and a diminishing love for the work one does.

Team Stage (n.d.) conducted a study in which they found that employees who are motivated are 87% less likely to resign from their positions. In that same study, they found that only 15% of employees around the world feel motivated. They also found that 81% of employees are considering resigning from their current position for a better offer.

Looking at those statistics alone, we can see that there are clearly issues with motivation worldwide.

WHAT IS MOTIVATION?

Motivation is what drives a person's every decision. Motivation is what triggers, controls, and sustains goal-oriented behaviors. Anything you do, you're almost always doing it with the motivation of satiating a desire, achieving a goal, or meeting a need. And when there is no motivation, there is always a desperate struggle to do the thing at all.

There are two main types of motivation: intrinsic and extrinsic.

Intrinsic motivation comes from inside you. It is an internal force that drives you, and usually it comes without any external recognition or rewards. For example, doing yoga to improve your mental health or doing art because it makes you happy.

Extrinsic motivation is when there is an external force—such as money, recognition, praise, rewards, and so on—that drives you. The motivation stems from a desire to receive that external reward.

As you can imagine, motivation is very important. Without it, nothing would get done—at least not properly. That's because motivation does more than trigger us into action; it also drives us to persistently and intensely pursue our goals. And this leads to greater and more passionate work.

There are a few things that an understanding of motivation can offer us. It can

- elevate your overall well-being and happiness.
- enhance your efficiency as you strive toward your goals.
- empower you to feel more in control of yourself and your life.

- drive you into taking action.
- aid you in avoiding unhealthy behaviors.
- foster healthy behaviors.

WHAT CAUSES A LACK OF MOTIVATION?

Why is there this massive motivation problem, then? The force that drives every human action—how does one lose such a thing?

- Fear: fears that you're not good enough, i.e., self-limiting beliefs that hold you back.
- Conflict in values: When you're working toward something that directly contradicts your values and passions, then you won't have any motivation to be successful in that venture.
- The wrong goals: Often, people set goals that do not motivate them appropriately. They're either goals that don't align with one's true passions, or they're goals that don't seem attainable because they're unclear or because there's no clear road toward that goal.
- Grief: Grief can impact us in many ways. One way is by making us question if "anything is worth it," and with that question looming over our heads, it can often lead to demotivation.
- Lack of challenge: Despite how often we complain about difficulties, humans regularly thrive under pressure. When there is no challenge—when there's no drive to overcome something—there is seldom motivation to take part at all.
- Burnout: Essentially, you're all out of motivation—you've used it all up.
- Lack of autonomy: When we're working toward something

that was decided for us, there can be no motivation to succeed.

- Lack of clarity: This points back to not having efficient goals. When there is no clarity on your vision or on the steps you need to take to get there, how can there be motivation?

THE RELATIONSHIP BETWEEN EMOTIONAL INTELLIGENCE AND BOOSTING MOTIVATION

Now that we understand the factors that contribute to a loss in motivation, we may be able to harness emotional intelligence to reaffirm, reestablish, and reinforce our motivation. All the tools and benefits that emotional intelligence offers us are ones we can use to boost our motivation or find it if we have lost it.

The first step has already been taken. You've gained an understanding of what motivation is and how it can be lost.

The second step has also been taken: learning where you are with your emotional intelligence. You've even taken the in-between step of starting to improve your EI by reading this book.

The third step involves learning what it takes to inspire others and yourself. This step involves learning more about motivation and productivity because the more you learn, the more insight you have and the more capability you have to put that information to good use.

The fourth step is involving yourself with others. Having others to encourage you is a great boon to your motivation.

The final step is ensuring that your environment is somewhere where your creativity and productivity can bloom. If your environment lends to your motivation, that's half the work done for you.

Emotional intelligence has a few key areas where it can help boost motivation:

- **Achievement drive**: As the name suggests, this is your drive to achieve. It can ebb and flow according to how much you believe your goal is within reach and whether or not you deserve it. The way to increase your achievement drive is to attach meaning to your goal. Remind yourself of all the whys of this goal.
- **Commitment**: Using EI to enhance your commitment involves preparing not to back down in the pursuit of your goal. It involves fending off procrastination and reflecting on how deep your desire for success runs.
- **Initiative**: Having initiative involves regulating your fear of failure. Initiative means putting in your all, doing more than you need to, and doing the very best you can.
- **Optimism**: Optimism is a great tool to achieve the other points in this list. Looking on the bright side of things and expecting the best of yourself, others, and the results is a great way to keep motivation high.

INTRINSIC MOTIVATION FOR ENHANCING YOUR EMOTIONAL INTELLIGENCE

The other aspect of this connection between EI and motivation is that it builds an intrinsic desire and motivation to improve one's emotional intelligence. Building one builds the other, and vice versa. Building both is the key to achieving personal and professional growth. There is an innate air of healthy development in a group that's got both high EI and motivation. Leaders are able to neutralize any disruptions, and employees are able to better understand their limits. Neither push too hard nor expect too much.

Furthermore, a good combination of EI and motivation leads to an optimistic and committed individual who takes initiative and drives themselves to achieve their goals. Individuals like this are not deterred by setbacks. They can overcome frustrations and fallouts. They take accountability. They're adaptable, and they're willing to regroup and try again. And really, what more could you ask for?

TIPS ON HOW TO GET MOTIVATED

If you're thinking, "That's great, but how is any of this supposed to help me increase my motivation?" Don't worry. All of this information is merely to provide insight into the complexities of motivation and what it has to do with emotional intelligence.

When it comes to actually increasing your motivation, I have some good news and some bad news. Because, you see, motivation is one of those things that is just so personal and unique to each individual. That means there can be no step-by-step guide on how to regain that motivation.

However, there are a few tips I can offer that significantly helped me and may set you on the right path.

The first tip is to set a great goal. What makes a great goal? A great goal is achievable, specific, and matches your values. A great goal has a time frame, and it can be broken down into smaller, actionable steps and tasks you can work through.

That right there is the second tip: breaking your goal into smaller tasks that are more attainable and not so overwhelming.

The third tip is to truly invest some time in finding better ways to achieve your goals. The first steps you come up with do not have to be set in stone. A plan toward a goal can adapt and grow, even if the goal stays the same.

The fourth tip is to take advantage of external sources of motivation, such as friends, family, partners, mentors, inspiration boards, daily reminders, and so on. Even though this is a self-development journey, it doesn't mean you have to do it all on your own. Let others encourage, remind, and motivate you, as well as hold you accountable.

LESSONS FROM JAY SHETTY

Jay Shetty, author of *Think Like a Monk,* said in a blog in 2020 that we are all motivated at our core by four main things: fear, desire, duty, and love.

Shetty says that figuring out which one of these four motivators is the driving force behind a goal is how we gain a clearer insight into where we are in life, where we'd like to go in life, and why. In order to find out which motivator is behind your goal, you must ask four questions:

- What is the ultimate aim of these plans and goals?
- What am I seeking through my choices?
- Am I pursuing a thrill or looking for safety and security?
- Am I trying to make an impact and live my life with purpose?

GETTING MOTIVATED AGAIN

Whether or not you're more of a write-your-feelings-down kind of person, I implore you to partake in the following activity in hopes of rediscovering your motivation. Remember what we said about writing earlier in this book. For each task you feel unmotivated to continue working on, fill out the following worksheet:

1. Name the Activity:

2. Were you motivated to do this activity at one point?

3. How did that feel?

4. When did you start feeling unmotivated?

5. How or why do you think that happened?

6. Can you think of a way to solve this problem?

7. What do you tell yourself when you are unmotivated about this activity?

8. What makes gaining back your motivation for this activity worth it? (Circle all that applies.)

    A. Money
    B. Prove myself capable
    C. Help others
    D. Achieve my goals
    E. Other. Name it:

9. If you were motivated, what would be your next steps toward completing the goal?

    A. Step 1:

B. Step 2:

C. Step 3:

D. Step 4:

10. If you get motivated again, can you think of a way to prevent your lack of motivation from taking hold again?

11. In question 7, I asked what you tell yourself when you're feeling unmotivated. If those words were to have come from an external source, what would your response to them be?

REGULATING THE ROLLERCOASTER

Reddit user, u/maybeitsmaybelean, posted in 2019 that the worst symptom of their ADHD diagnosis was emotional dysregulation. Emotional dysregulation is a serious challenge that many people face, and it can make it feel like controlling our emotions is akin to catching a feather in a hurricane.

Do you ever feel like that? Do you ever feel like trying to chill out when you're stressed is like swimming against the tide? Do you ever feel like trying to calm down when you're angry is like trying to snuff a firework? Do you ever feel like trying to cheer yourself up when you're upset is like trying to stop the moon from rising?

You're not alone. Within this chapter, you'll hopefully find a coping mechanism to help.

EMOTIONAL SELF-REGULATION

Emotional dysregulation is when an emotional response is uncontrolled and does not abide by the traditionally accepted range of emotional reactions. Emotional dysregulation can include mood swings and mood lability—rapid, and often exaggerated, changes in emotions.

Symptoms of emotional dysregulation include

- outbursts of anger
- anxiety
- severe depression
- self-harm ideation or attempts
- shame
- perfectionism
- unusual conflict in relationships
- eating disorders
- suicide ideation or attempts
- other self-damaging behaviors

There are a few things that are believed to cause emotional dysregulation, such as traumatic brain injuries, constant invalidation of one's thoughts and feelings, early childhood trauma, or childhood neglect.

There are some treatments that are regularly used to try to minimize the effect of emotional dysregulation on patients:

- professional counseling
- antidepressant medications
- treating the underlying conditions and causes
- diet and exercise

- emotional regulation techniques
- psychological tools that promote positive self-esteem

Emotional Regulation

In contrast to emotional dysregulation, emotional regulation entails the ability to control one's emotions and behaviors. Specifically, it entails the ability to control disruptive emotions and behaviors. Emotional regulation starts in childhood but, if not mastered within adulthood, can lead to much harsher consequences. It starts in children, with the ability to

- concentrate on one task.
- manage strong emotions.
- calm oneself down after becoming angry or excited.
- behave in helpful and cooperative ways.
- control one's impulses.

Despite the term, emotional regulation consists of more than just being able to control your emotions. A large aspect of emotional regulation is your ability to control your behavior and reactions, despite your emotions. Emotional regulation may be calming yourself down, but it may also be behaving calmly despite feeling frustrated.

To gain a better insight into emotional regulation and all its facets, let's have a look at what scholars and psychologists have to say on the matter.

- In 2007, Roy Baumeister proposed the self-regulation theory, which states that there are four components involved with self-regulation that interact to determine our self-regulatory activity. These four components are:

○ our personal standards of desirable behavior
○ our motivation to meet those standards
○ monitoring the consequences of breaking those standards
○ our willpower to control our urges
In 1991, Albert Bandura explained that self-regulation is an active process in which we are responsible for
○ monitoring our own behavior, the consequences of that behavior, and what is influencing our behavior.
○ judging our own behavior in relation to our personal standards and the standards of others and the environment.
○ reacting to our own behavior.

- Self-regulated learning is a concept originally coined by B.J. Zimmerman in 1986. It refers to a process whereby a student takes responsibility for their own learning. This process includes three steps.

○ Step 1: Planning. This involves setting goals, planning actionable steps, creating schedules, and studying strategies.
○ Step 2: Monitoring. This involves putting the plans into action and monitoring one's own performance. It also involves learning from experience which strategies are most efficient.
○ Step 3: Reflection. This involves reflecting on the strategies and the results. It also involves ruminating on how well one believes they did and why.

- The self-regulatory model is believed to offer a better

understanding of self-regulation theory. The model is somewhat of a cycle and follows this progression:

- ○ The presentation of stimuli.
- ○ The stimuli are registered both emotionally and cognitively. In other words, stimuli are understood and felt.
- ○ Once the stimuli are made sense of, an individual chooses a coping response.
- ○ The combination of making sense of the stimuli and finding a response to said stimuli creates an outcome.
- ○ The individual evaluates their response according to the outcome and must choose whether to stick with that coping response or develop a new one.

- In 2014, R.F. Baumeister proposed that an important concept of self-regulation theory is ego depletion or self-regulatory depletion. This defines a state in which one's ability to self-regulate has been depleted—their willpower, control, and energy have been expended. This results in poor behavior and decision-making. Ego depletion may be responsible for our moments of weakness. It may explain why even those with superb emotional intelligence struggle to control themselves sometimes.

Types of Self-Regulation

There are a few different kinds of self-regulation. Gaining a better understanding of these types of self-regulation may inspire some reflection or the implementation of similar techniques in your own life.

- Self-monitoring: keeping track of one's progress, usually in the form of recording the results of the outcome. This is a great way to see your improvement over time.
- Self-instruction: talking oneself through a task. This can be used in all types of situations, for example:

  ○ Initiating a task: "The first step is to…"
  ○ Coping during a difficult situation: "Stay calm. I must just find a solution. It's not their fault."
  ○ Self-evaluating: "How could I explain this in a different way so I know I understand?"
  ○ Rewarding oneself: "Yes! Now I get to play video games until dinner."

- Goal-setting: creating clear, achievable goals with an actionable plan to achieve them.
- Self-reinforcement: encouraging yourself after accomplishing something. Acknowledge when you've done something that the "before" you wouldn't have done, like choosing not to flip off the guy who cut you off in traffic this morning.

Managing Your Emotions

Not everyone is built to be a manager. However, we are each responsible for managing our own emotions. I don't know what could be more difficult than managing something that is notoriously untamed and unwieldy. Even the best managers with the best control over their emotions, can sometimes snap.

Thankfully, because it's so important, there are tried and true methods of wrangling one's emotions that may be helpful:

- Explore and find alternative and healthy ways to express your emotions. The term "expressing" one's emotions may be confusing for some, but the idea is to allow the emotion to be felt without ruining your day, whether that be journaling, sketching, venting to a friend, playing darts, running, or whatever works for you.
- Practice giving yourself space to regulate your emotions. It is seldom that a situation cannot spare five minutes for you to separate yourself from the situation and find your head again.
- Acknowledge what makes you feel good and what calms you down. Recognize what triggers positive emotions for you.
- Practice staying in the present moment. Explore mindfulness techniques that help you develop a new perspective on your emotions and situations.
- Track and journal your emotions. Being able to reflect on previous emotions can help us put our current emotions into perspective.
- Explore breathing techniques. Proper breathing exercises can be extremely useful in regulating one's emotions. I have experienced the astounding effect that deep breaths can have on your physiological state.
- Consider seeking professional help. Licensed therapists are well-studied on the topic of emotional regulation. They will help you with techniques to improve your emotional regulation, but they may also help you address the underlying issues that make it particularly difficult.

And, while we're on the topic of healthy and effective emotional regulation methods, I wanted to touch on a few harmful methods that you may be using. You may think you've got a hold on your emotions, but using one of these methods is harmful to yourself. Forgive yourself for what you've done in the past, and strive to do better in the future.

- denial
- substance abuse
- withdrawal
- self-harm
- bullying

Essential Emotional Regulation Skills to Have

The journey from actively managing one's emotions to having passive emotional regulation skills is a pivotal one. Learning to tame your emotions eliminates the hold they have over you. Having these skills gives you the confidence to know that, when faced with challenges, you are able to remain resilient and maintain a healthy emotional balance. These skills include the ability to

- identify the specific emotions you're feeling.
- identify the specific emotions others are feeling—further than simply labeling them as being in a "bad mood."
- soothe your own emotions.
- soothe others' emotions.
- have intimate and difficult conversations.
- commit to and persevere toward your goals.
- remain strong under external pressure.
- tolerate awkwardness and silence.
- control one's impulsive behaviors.
- regulate positive emotions, not only negative ones.

The Eight Cs and Five Ps for a Higher Self

In the pursuit of self-improvement, it truly helps to have a comprehensive approach. In his work as the founder of Internal Family Systems Therapy, Richard Schwartz found that there are several significant parts to one's "self." Actively working on refining and improving each of these parts can be the basis of your approach to self-improvement (Laurence, 2023).

- curiosity
- confidence
- calmness
- clarity
- compassion
- courage
- connectedness
- creativity
- presence
- patience
- playfulness
- persistence
- perspective

SELF-CONTROL

In 2016, Stuart Shanker explained that there exists a difference between self-regulation and self-control. Although the terms are very similar, Shanker suggests that the difference lies in our approach to strong impulses. Self-control aims to inhibit them, while self-regulation is about minimizing the frequency and intensity of these impulses. Self-regulation also approaches this in a different way. Rather than approaching the impulses directly, self-regulation addresses stress load and recovery. According to Shanker, self-control is only possible through self-regulation, and, in many cases, it is rendered unnecessary (Ackerman, 2018b).

However, until one masters self-regulation, self-control is still a useful skill to possess. Self-control is the ability to increase desirable behaviors and manage your responses to undesirable ones. There are three primary types of self-control:

- Emotional control is everything we have spoken about up until this point.
- Impulse control is the ability to manage one's impulses and urges.
- Movement control is the ability to manage when and how one's body moves; a lack of movement control may result in unwanted fidgeting and restlessness.

Delayed gratification is an important element of self-control, specifically impulse control. Delayed gratification means waiting to get whatever you desire. This technique involves prioritizing long-term rewards over short-term desires. This can be an efficient method of self-control when we remind ourselves that a moment's self-control will lead to bigger rewards later. For example, you may want to buy yourself lunch to fuel your stress-eating habits. However, you know that if you save that money, it can instead go toward that new TV you want to purchase at the end of the year.

When asked what factors were keeping them from achieving their goals, the APA (2011) found that 27% of respondents said that a lack of willpower was the primary factor. A good sense of self-control can lead to a happier and more satisfying lifestyle, as well as, a healthier one. It's true—self-control has been shown to result in a lowered likelihood of developing

- airflow obstruction.
- metabolic abnormalities.
- sexually transmitted infections.
- elevated inflammation.
- periodontal disease.
- substance dependence.

It may seem too good to be true, but if you truly think about it, there are many health problems that can be caused by risky and unhealthy behaviors. Self-control minimizes those behaviors and, therefore, the likelihood of behavior-caused health problems as well.

Self-Control Techniques

The following techniques can be put into practice while learning and developing your self-control. Remember that practice makes perfect, and it's okay to make mistakes when you're just starting out and even when you've been at it for a while.

- Plan ahead for situations that may make you lose your self-control. For example, I often drink a lot of caffeine before bed. I'd like to stop that behavior, so I must amend my sleeping patterns to be healthier.
- Avoid the temptation as much as you can. For example, don't keep caffeinated drinks in the house.
- Focus on one goal at a time. For example, while trying to give up caffeine, don't try to give up sugar at the same time. Remember ego depletion? That remains true with self-control, and focusing on too many goals at once will expend your willpower faster.
- Put your self-control into practice. A great way to deter ego depletion is to regularly build that self-control muscle. For

example, when you're out at a restaurant and you *could* treat yourself to a caffeinated drink, opt for something else instead.

- Meditate on the new behavior you want to begin and the good results it will yield. You must control your breathing, your mind, and your body.
- Remind yourself of the consequences of losing your self-control. For example, caffeine ruins my healthy sleeping patterns and is bad for my heart.

HOW CELEBS REGULATE THEIR EMOTIONS

Emotional regulation is not just for the average person. Everyone needs to be able to regulate their emotions to live a fulfilling and chaos-free lifestyle—even celebrities. In fact, when your career rides on your reputation, keeping a cool head is essential.

Surprisingly enough, celebrities regulate their emotions and manage their mental health in much the same way as we do. When asked about this topic, many celebrities advocate the importance of self-care, healthy sleeping habits, healthy eating habits, and mindfulness.

Camila Cabello told Slice (Palbom, 2021) that when she struggled with mental health while working on "Million to One," she found a way to cope by focusing her efforts on her music and acting. Here we can, again, see how motivation goes hand-in-hand with emotional intelligence. A deep passion for something can often be our anchor to calmness and control.

In the same article, former First Lady Michelle Obama offered a different piece of advice for dealing with overwhelming emotions. For Mrs. Obama, her family and friends are her anchor. When everything becomes too much for her, she knows she can count on her support system to help her get her head back on her shoulders.

While doing my research for this book, I was truly moved by an article by Romper (2021) that I came across that discussed how actress Kristen Bell teaches her children emotional regulation. I was impressed by her awareness that, regardless of fame and fortune, parents are still responsible for teaching their children these complex lessons.

When Bell's children are trying to navigate "big emotions," she always asks them one question: "Do you want a solution for the problem you're crying about, or do you just want to let this feeling pass you?" This is part of a deeper lesson Bell is teaching her daughters, where they are to acknowledge that they are not defined by their feelings. Instead, their feelings are only something that is passing through them.

Bell reminds herself of this lesson in times of distress and will even separate herself from distressing situations for 10 minutes so that she is able to regulate herself and return to the situation with a clear mind.

STOPP STRATEGY FOR REGULATING EMOTIONS

Practicing emotional regulation in real time can be monumentally challenging. In moments where you can feel your hold on your emotions slipping, there is a method you can use to regain control. The STOPP strategy is a blend of cognitive behavioral therapy, dialectical behavior therapy, and mindfulness that helps us acknowledge and control our emotions in the heat of the moment.

STOPP is an acronym that stands for the following:

- **Stop** and take a moment to compose yourself.
- **Take** a breath and practice calming breathing techniques.
- **Observe** your thoughts, emotions, and situation. Ask yourself:

  o What are you thinking right now?
  o Where are you focusing your attention?
  o What sensations are you feeling in your body?
  o What are you reacting to?
  o Is what I am feeling directly related to what happened or to something else?

- **Perspective.** Pull back from the situation and try to look at it from a different perspective. Ask yourself:

  o If I asked a friend for advice right now, what would they say?
  o Is there another way to see this situation?
  o What level of importance does this hold?
  o What level of importance will this hold in 10 minutes, 10 hours, or 10 months' time?
  o Am I reacting to a fact or an opinion?
  o Is there a more reasonable explanation?

- **Proceed** with the best course of action for yourself and others. Proceed with the course of action that is most appropriate and that best aligns with your personal values.

THE RIGHT ATTENTION

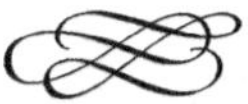

In her book, *Just Listen*, Sarah Dessen (2012) describes a good listener as someone who doesn't jump in on your sentences under the guise of saving you from having to actually finish them. A good listener is someone who doesn't talk over you, effectively rendering the information you can get out lost and altered. A good listener waits for you to keep going.

However, it doesn't help to listen well if you're not paying attention. Attention skills are just as important as listening skills, and they often go hand-in-hand with one another. Improving one will ultimately improve the other.

Attention is also a key aspect of emotional intelligence, specifically self-awareness and inner focus. Meta-awareness, also referred to as meta-cognition or meta-emotion, enables us to observe our internal realm instead of being controlled by it. Unfortunately, the world we live in today is not built to foster and improve attention. There is always something looking to seduce our focus away from what it needs to be on.

Attention skills and active listening habits are not just for partners and students. They are the glue behind every communication skill and interpersonal relationship. Learning these two skills will act as a boon in every life situation.

ATTENTION

Attention is the cognitive ability to actively process specific information while filtering out irrelevant details. I don't know about you, but I've always found this extremely difficult, particularly when the irrelevant details seem to be much more interesting than the important information.

Attention acts much like a highlighter, directing our focus and interest to particular areas of interest.

However, attention doesn't only involve narrowing our focus; it also involves disregarding stimuli that are competing for our concentration. Attentional resources have a limited capacity and duration. It's because of this that managing our attention is so important.

By selectively tuning out unimportant sensations, information, and perceptions, we are better equipped to understand the most important information given to us.

There are five different types of attention. They are as follows:

- **Sustained attention**: Also referred to as concentration, the skill to maintain focus on a single task for a prolonged duration. This is the type of attention used while studying, for instance.
- **Selective attention**: This is the ability to selectively manage our attentional resources among several stimuli.

This ability requires the capability to block out internal and external stimuli that aren't important. This is the type of attention used to read while music is playing.

- **Alternating attention**: Also known as multi-tasking, this is the ability to effortlessly shift one's attention between two or more cognitive demands. Importantly, this is not the ability to focus on two things at once; instead, it involves stopping attending to one thing in order to attend to another. This type of attention is commonly used by mothers in their daily tasks.

- **Limited attention**: Also known as divided attention, this is the ability to divide our attention among multiple tasks or stimuli. This is the type of attention used when driving a car, for instance.

- **Focused attention**: This is the ability to refocus our attention on new and sudden stimuli. This ability allows us to rapidly respond to changing external stimuli. This type of attention is used in sports and video games.

Finding a balance in attention is crucial, as extremes in either direction can be problematic. It is important to avoid both overly narrow focus and attention that is too widely dispersed, as they can disrupt our performance.

A state of "flow" is considered to be ideal. When you are fully engrossed in a task and facing a challenge, that's the state of complete absorption. Being fully engrossed in a task like this makes drowning out irrelevant stimuli much easier, including negative self-talk! Productive and confident time spent is always ideal.

However, the opposite of "flow" also exists, and we've all experienced it at one point or another. Instead of being engrossed by a productive task, we're overtaken by an emotional trigger and can't do or think about much else.

There is a proven relationship between our attention and emotions (Pessoa, 2010). There is a certain amount of attention needed to process our emotions, especially when those emotions are "irrelevant" or "unimportant" to the task at hand. When the attention needed for a task is low, the rest of our attentional resources can focus on processing emotional stimuli. However, when the task at hand requires more attention, there are fewer and fewer resources available for processing those emotional stimuli. When we reach our attentional capacity, emotional perception may disappear altogether.

This is why we may struggle to identify, understand, and manage emotions when we're too narrowly focused on a task. This is when we snap, become stressed, and lose our self-control.

This is why strengthening our attention skills is so vital, because we can avoid being emotionally hijacked like this. Improving our ability to allocate, maintain, and manage our attention offers us more attentional capacity to ensure our emotional intelligence is not forgotten.

LISTENING

Listening goes beyond simply hearing sounds; it involves receiving, understanding, evaluating, and responding to the messages conveyed through those sounds. Good listeners are able to comprehend what they hear and respond appropriately.

What makes a good listener?

- They always aim to fully comprehend what's being told to them. They will ask for clarifying details if necessary.
- They are able to interpret not only what is being said but also nonverbal cues like body language and tone of voice.
- They show curiosity about what is being shared and ask questions.
- They listen actively. We will get into this topic more in a bit, but for now, know that active listening consists of two components:

  ○ Paying attention to who's giving you the message and showing that attention is given. They show this by holding eye contact, nodding, sitting upright, and mirroring body language.
  ○ Reflecting on and responding to the message. You can show that you've understood what you've been told by paraphrasing the information and allowing the messenger to correct anything you've misunderstood.

So, listening requires attentiveness and comprehension. Since both of those factors operate on more of a scale than a strict on/off switch, that means that different levels of attentiveness and comprehension lend to different levels of listening. There are five different levels of listening:

- **Ignoring**: This doesn't truly count as listening. There is no attentiveness and no comprehension. This is never an appropriate level of listening.
- **Pretend listening**: As the name suggests, this is when you're showing all the signs of listening (such as body language), but you aren't actually listening. Once again, this is never an appropriate level because once we're asked

questions or asked to act on what was said, we will be caught out.

- **Selective listening**: Similar to pretend listening, however, we do engage with certain parts of the messages—usually only the parts that interest us. And, similar to pretend listening, when we're asked to act on what we heard, we will be caught out.
- **Attentive listening**: This is good and active listening. It is appropriate in every situation.
- **Empathic listening**: This goes a step beyond active listening. Empathic listening is when we strive to understand not only the words of the messenger but also their perspective. We try to understand why the message is important and how it's meant to make us feel.

How to Improve Your Listening Skills

Would you say you're a good and active listener? Which of the five levels of listening are you most often partaking in? Does it change depending on who's speaking? If so, why? Learning more about the way we listen can really help us get that "before" image when we first start our self-improvement journey. So, if you feel like listening may be a weakness that hasn't yet hit the gym, here are some workouts to try.

Practice

- being fully present. They're completely engaged and focused on the present conversation.
- listening, not for the sake of responding. Yes, a conversation is back-and-forth, but if you spend the entire

time thinking about how you will respond, you'll never actually hear what is being told to you.

- reacting in the moment. Listening is not about responding; it's about understanding what you've heard and reacting to the information. However, many people go into "planning mode" after receiving new information rather than reacting with their gut instinct. Responding to information when you're present and, in the moment, can foster better relationships with the messenger.
- not offering advice at every turn. Sometimes, "fixing" the problem is not what's needed. Sometimes, all that's needed is to get your emotions off your chest. All you need to do is listen.
- not interrupting. That's it. Don't interrupt. Ever.
- not having an agenda when you enter a conversation. Try going into a conversation without expecting any certain outcome. This way, you won't steer the conversation in any direction and can gladly let the messenger take the initiative.
- listening more than you speak. And when you do speak, respond appropriately—ask questions or provide support or encouragement. Don't dominate the conversation.
- asking follow-up or clarifying questions. Don't be content with not understanding or only half understanding what was said.
- listening to learn something. Ask open-ended questions to let the messenger elaborate.
- showing that you're listening. Use eye contact, nodding, and body language to let the messenger know they have your undivided attention.
- patience. Even when you're ready to say your piece or end

the conversation, allow the messenger to finish what they're saying first.

- differentiating between fact and opinion. Knowing the difference can provide insight into whether or not the messenger is delivering a factual or subjective message. This can change how you understand and react to the information.
- opening yourself up to new ideas. Go into conversations with an open mind and be receptive to messages, regardless of whether they benefit you or align with what you already believe.
- letting go of assumptions. Don't go into a conversation with your mind made up about what type of person the messenger is, what type of message they will be sharing, or what you will learn from the interaction.
- taking notes. Notes aren't only for classes and meetings. The important thing to remember with note-taking is to be concise and selective. Don't stop listening to focus on finishing the sentence.
- relying on your reason and common sense. Active listening doesn't mean blindly listening without reason. If a message does not sound logical, credible, or coherent, then respond accordingly and appropriately.
- relating new information to old information. Often, we go into conversations with a firm set of beliefs and only listen to that which bolsters them. However, when you're doing this, you're not truly listening. Be sure to take in all the information and, while processing it, see how and if it relates to your beliefs.

The Benefits of Improving Your Listening Skills

By taking the time to improve your listening skills, you can readily tap into the many benefits that come with being a good listener.

- Better comprehension leads to better results. This will make you a better student, worker, colleague, and teammate. You'll be able to pick up on what's important and what's expected of you, and you'll be in a great position to deliver results.
- Due to your increased ability to deliver great results, you will be perceived as more intelligent and perceptive. Reputation is a great boon to have, especially in the business world.
- Having good listening skills is something many people are looking for in a partner and a friend. Showing your friends undivided attention is an act of love they will notice and remember.
- Being a good listener can help you become a good public speaker. Active listening will teach you what listeners look for and pay attention to. You'll have the "inside scoop" on what it takes to hold an audience's attention.

Different Listening Styles

Everyone can benefit from improving their listening skills, but not everyone has the same style of listening, nor is every style of listening appropriate or effective in every situation. Good listening skills include knowing which listening style to use in which situation. There are four styles to choose from.

- **People-oriented listening**: The main priority is the speaker. The message is an avenue for gaining better insight into how the speaker thinks and feels about their message. You may ask questions like "What is the speaker's history in this subject?" or "Do they feel successful?"
- **Content-oriented listening**: The main priority is the message itself. The listener is determining whether or not the message is accurate. Many listeners are content-oriented listeners, and, as such, speakers have an obligation to share accurate information.
- **Action-oriented listening**: The main priority is identifying what the speaker wants. Do they want the listeners' votes, actions, volunteers, donations, interest, or something else? This style of listening can also be called task-oriented listening. While listening, you're actively seeking the message of what needs to be done.
- **Time-oriented listening**: The main priority is getting to the point quickly. These listeners are not interested in fluff and unnecessary background information. They prefer concise information. These types of listeners are usually obvious in their impatience.

ACTIVE LISTENING

Active listening is the best type of listening that one can offer a speaker because you're offering them the respect they deserve. It's also the best listening you can do for yourself. You hear more of the message—more than just the words being said. Actively listening helps develop deep and meaningful relationships because, around you, people feel heard. These deep connections really improve your judgment of character.

After discussing how important attention is, active listening involves directly practicing that muscle. Active listening is so important; it is one of the basic things toddlers are taught at school. When I was teaching kindergarten classes, one of our primary lessons involved teaching children how to listen. Active listening is what they teach. They teach it using the five Ls of listening and learning, which include:

- ears that are listening
- eyes that are looking
- lips that are shut tight
- hands that are in their lap
- legs that are crossed

These five Ls foster minimal distractive behaviors that may take away from a toddler's ability to listen attentively and actively. However, for adults, teaching active listening cannot be so simple. These five Ls offer a rudimentary basis, but, seeing as we're not toddlers, we can go a step further. In fact, we can go two steps further and turn those five Ls into seven techniques.

- Paraphrasing is a technique where you restate the information you receive to confirm with the speaker that you've understood correctly. Doing this encourages the speaker to continue and lets them know you're interested in what they have to say.
- Verbalizing your emotions is another way to convey your interest and even help the speaker verbalize their own emotions.
- Be sure to ask for more information if you need it.
- Summarize the information you've received. This creates

an opening for further conversation and helps to pull together the important points of the conversation.

- Clarifying what you've heard can help both you and the speaker see the perspective of the other side. This fosters further and deeper conversation.
- Encourage the speaker to continue speaking—bring up alternative information and offer ideas and other suggestions.
- Balance the conversation by adding your own thoughts and perspectives and helping the speaker evaluate their own feelings on the matter.

STANDING OUT WITH YOUR SOCIAL SKILLS

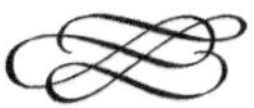

In his 2015 book, *Overachievement*, John Eliot wrote:

> Genuine confidence is a way of thinking about yourself and your abilities. Confidence is your perception of your own potential; it's a kind of long-term thinking that powers you through the obstacles and tough times, helping you solve problems and putting you in the way of success. Your confidence is quite a separate matter from your social skills.
> (p. 139)

In the landscape of self-development, genuine confidence acts as an anchor that grounds individuals in a strong sense of belief in their own capabilities. However, in the landscape of social interactions and relationships, the link between social skills and emotional intelligence is equally significant. While genuine confidence reflects one's self-perception, the mastery of social intricacies and emotional cues significantly influences relationships, success, and well-being.

WHAT ARE SOCIAL SKILLS?

Much like relationships and communication and listening and attention work together, emotional intelligence and social skills are two sides of the same coin. Like so many aspects discussed in this book, improving one indirectly improves others. Social skills promote effective communication in any interpersonal relationship and even in random encounters.

Social skills are not only verbal. It expands to written, nonverbal, and visual communication as well. Social skills are exercised in the

- language you use.
- gestures you make.
- tone, pitch, and volume of your voice.
- eye contact you maintain.
- facial expressions you make.
- body language you use.

WHAT ARE THE ADVANTAGES OF SOCIAL SKILLS?

Social skills are taught to us from a very young age. We are always encouraged to interact and socialize because, throughout our lives, we are regularly practicing those muscles. The more actively we pursue improvement in the realm of social skills, the more benefits we are open to receiving.

- Improved relationships. Not only will we be able to make more friends, but we will also be able to maintain and build on the relationships that are important to us. We will be better within those relationships, offering our loved ones better experiences and connections.

- Time can be better spent with people you love. Greater social skills give you the benefit of knowing who you no longer want to invest time in. It's healthy to remove yourself from people who don't contribute positively to your life in any way. With greater social skills, you will also be more adept at politely letting those people know that you want to spend time with other people.
- Greater social skills truly put us in an advantageous position in the workplace—mainly through having great relationships with clients, colleagues, and superiors. Many jobs have a "people component," and when we are more adept at that component, work life can be easier and more fulfilling.
- Better communication skills. Communication plays such an important role in so many aspects of life, and, therefore, anything that improves our communication skills is incredibly important.

IMPORTANCE OF SOCIAL SKILLS

Beyond just the benefits, social skills are incredibly important in our day-to-day lives. Social skills play a pivotal role in many facets of our lives, improving and making things easier for us. Good social skills

- promote dialogue among peers.
- increase understanding and empathy.
- are necessary to be a part of social groups.
- are the foundation for positive interpersonal relationships.
- are extremely important for health and longevity.
- allow you to convey the right emotions in the right way.

- make or break business deals, relationships, or conversations.
- help to initiate contact and carry it to higher levels of relationships.
- improve how likeable you are to those around you.
- help to implement and maintain healthy boundaries.

HOW TO IMPROVE SOCIAL SKILLS

Now, don't worry. I'm not going to sell you on social skills and how important they are without offering you some tools that will help you improve your own social skills. Social skills are particularly tricky to navigate because they are so intricately intertwined with other people—other people whom we have no control over. Here are some ways to improve your social skills.

- Regularly exercise the muscle. Engage with other people. Join in-person or online community groups. Go out. Participate in meetings.
- Practice letting others talk more, and encourage them to do so. Ask open-ended questions that encourage people to freely express their thoughts, emotions, opinions, and experiences.
- Observe others' social skills. Much can be learned through observation. Look around you and take note of people's questions, body language, tone of voice, and vocabulary. Incorporate some of the positive things you observe into your own skill set.
- Start small. Try responding with questions rather than one-word statements next time you talk to a stranger. Lengthen conversations rather than trying to cut them off early.

- One skill you can practice in every interaction is eye contact. It's a great way to show that you're invested in the conversation and what the other person has to say.
- Compliment people openly and regularly.
- Practice good listening skills.
- Don't be afraid to develop relationships further. Build friendships with colleagues, acquaintances, and family members. Invest in those relationships.
- Keep up with current events and trends. Be "in" on what everyone is currently interested in so as to take part in the conversation.

PERSUASION

Persuasion: the art of convincing someone else to agree with an idea or to execute an action. Persuasion is all about articulating your ideas compellingly. Being able to get people on board with your ideas is a great social skill to have.

Here are a few examples of how persuasion is used in everyday life:

- Advertising and marketing. Businesses are always trying to persuade us to use their services or buy their products.
- Large-scale campaigns that build awareness for social causes persuade us to donate, volunteer, and share information.
- Salespeople persuade us to support their business.
- Speeches, articles, and inspirational videos persuade us to change our thinking on a topic.
- Team managers persuade us to work toward a common goal with vigor and enthusiasm.

- Teachers, lecturers, mentors, and counselors persuade us to engage with the information they have to share and use it to our advantage.
- Business owners and high-level managers persuade others to do business with them.

Persuasion is a social skill that challenges us to share our ideas in a way that gets other people on board. This takes time to perfect, but you can improve your persuasion skills. Here are a few methods to try:

- Take the time to enhance your communication skills. We will discuss communication skills next!
- Practice good listening skills. This will help establish trust with people you talk to, opening the door for them to hear you out about your ideas.
- Build on your emotional intelligence. And hey, you're more than halfway there! Evaluating and reacting to someone's emotions allows you to customize your persuasion style to best impact the person you're talking to.
- A great way to build your argument is to make use of logical and reasonable information. Sharing verifiable and credible facts ensures that your information is reliable.
- Build and nurture your interpersonal skills. Engage with people and maintain relationships with them. It's easier to sell an idea to someone with whom you've built a rapport.
- Learn the art of negotiation. Showing people the benefits of following your ideas is a great way to convince them. Learn what interests someone, and make sure to adjust your persuasion style accordingly.

COMMUNICATION

Communication is truly the core of any social skill. Building one's communication skills is a surefire and effective way to ultimately improve every other social skill. Simply put, communication is the act of transferring information from one person, place, or group to another. Communication involves three parts: the sender, the recipient, and the information itself. Each of these parts can be externally influenced, as can the relationships between them.

There are four main categories of communication:

- Verbal: information conveyed through the spoken word.
- Non-verbal: information conveyed through body language, style, gestures, and actions.
- Written: information conveyed through e-mails, letters, advertisements, literature, and so on.
- Visual: information conveyed through imagery, graphs, charts, logos, etc.

Improving your connection skills is one way to automatically improve almost every facet of your life. In my opinion, communication is the highest priority factor in any interpersonal relationship. Here are a few methods to enhance your communication skills:

- Adjust for the recipient. Not everyone communicates in the same way, so be sure to adapt to what works best for the recipient.
- Keep it concise. Don't overload your message with fancy and unnecessary words. Get to the point.
- Involve the recipient in telling the message. Let them share their experiences, feelings, opinions, and thoughts.

- Always use the best method to deliver the message. Adjust the communication style to match the intended message. Don't rush. Plan and execute.
- Read and use nonverbal communication to your advantage.
- As far as possible, do it face-to-face. It's easier to put all the skills you've learned thus far into action.
- Eye contact. Eye contact. Eye contact.
- Ask the recipient for feedback to better adjust your future communication.

SOCIAL LEADERSHIP

We've spoken about leadership a few times throughout this book. Even those of you who aren't in a leadership role can benefit from having leadership skills. Even when we're not in a leadership position, we can still strive to possess social leadership skills.

Social leadership involves recognizing the "we"—the team that is responsible for the creation and execution of ideas and decisions. Social leadership is all about developing connectivity within the community. It involves intuition, collaboration, vulnerability, care, empathy, courage, resilience, and self-awareness. Furthermore, it's important to remember that being right and having all the answers are not the goal. The goal is to be available to listen and offer empathic advice.

The most crucial factor in social leadership is focus. It allows for better engagement, empathy, and collaboration. Proactively prioritizing focus can minimize burnout, low morale, and dissatisfaction. However, there must always be a balance between focusing on work and focusing on people so as to enhance your leadership skills as well as your team's productivity.

This doesn't have to mean workplace teams. Perhaps there is a home improvement project that you and your family are working on. Social leadership can help that project run smoothly. Maybe you and your friends are playing games, fishing, or working together on a project; social leadership skills will help you there too. Social leadership skills simply aid you in keeping a group of people cooperative.

CONFLICT MANAGEMENT

I've always been deeply bothered by conflict. So much so, in fact, that I would often avoid it altogether. I used to avoid people who were arguing with each other, and I would avoid confronting anyone close to me who did me wrong out of fear of conflict.

However, in my years, I have learned that the best way to minimize conflict is not to avoid it but instead to manage it. Resolving conflict is like using a dustpan and throwing the trash away instead of sweeping everything under the rug only to have it resurface on a windy day.

Conflict management skills improve how conflict affects you and allow conflict to be a productive part of the work day—where it is accepted, managed, and used to the advantage of everyone.

Conflict management skills include skills we have already learned about in this book and new skills too!

- active listening.
- empathy.
- self-control and maintaining a level head.
- positivity.
- problem-solving.

Like most things, conflict management skills can be trained and practiced until they become second nature. However, it is a largely complex topic that could fill a whole book on its own. Improved conflict management skills require collaboration and practice. Learning from professionals is the most effective way to enhance your conflict management abilities. Sign up for classes or workshops hosted by professionals who can provide the tools you need to efficiently manage conflict. These workshops often include role-play activities. Be sure to collaborate with your partners and ask for feedback to improve as much as you can.

You'll be resolving conflict with ease soon enough!

LEARNING THE CUES

For some, identifying social cues comes as second nature. For others, it takes a conscious effort to recognize and make sense of social cues. Social cues offer us a plethora of information, which is incredibly useful in fully understanding and engaging with the other person.

Here are a few questions to ask during an interaction to help you recognize social cues:

- Are they maintaining eye contact? Eye contact, or the lack thereof, is one of the most active and important social cues to exist. It's indicative of how engaged and comfortable someone is during an interaction.
- Which way are they facing? People will face you directly when they are open to and comfortable with the conversation. If they are facing away, they may be uncomfortable.

- Are their arms crossed? People are likely to cross their arms when they're uncomfortable or distressed. Crossed arms are usually indicative of someone being closed off.
- How close are they standing to you? Is it an environmental or an active choice? If someone is slowly getting further away, it's likely that they are not engaged in the conversation.
- What does their posture reveal? Do they seem tired or excited?
- What do facial expressions tell you? Sometimes, our facial expressions subconsciously reveal how engaged we are in a conversation.
- Are they mirroring your body language? If they are, this is a good sign that they are matching your energy and are engaged with what you're saying.
- How are they smiling? Is it genuine or half-hearted?
- How are they dressed? If it is relevant to the situation, does it reveal how they view this interaction?
- Are they disengaged?

  - Are they looking down at their phone?
  - Are they sighing or yawning?
  - Are they distracted?
  - Are they not actively participating in the conversation?
  - Are they fidgeting?

- What is their tone? In person, tone is easier to pick up on than in texts, but it's still important to try and gauge what someone's tone says about their feelings and opinions.
- How loud are they talking? Volume can be indicative of how enthusiastic and engaged someone is.

- Are they touching you? Not everyone is touchy-feely, but when someone engages in physical touch, it's a good sign that they like you or what you're saying.

4-STEP GRADED EXPOSURE THERAPY FOR SOCIAL SKILLS

Exposure therapy involves exposing yourself to something that frightens or distresses you with the hope of confronting and overcoming it. When something distresses or frightens us, we are wont to avoid it at all costs. However, avoidance doesn't lend itself to overcoming fears and stressors.

Graded exposure involves creating a safe environment in which one can expose oneself in an effort to reduce fear and distress.

This is the 4-Step graded exposure therapy:

- **Step 1:** Make a list of situations that you're scared or distressed by. For example, public speaking.
- **Step 2:** Rate how scared or distressed you are by each of the listed items on a scale of one to ten. For example, public speaking=9 and making an appointment=7
- **Step 3:** Using the scores, order the items from most feared to least feared.
- **Step 4:** Start by exposing yourself to the least-feared item and work your way up to the most-feared item.

HOW EMOTIONAL INTELLIGENCE IMPACTS ALL YOUR RELATIONSHIPS

There are two main areas of our lives where emotional intelligence has the biggest impact on ourselves and our relationships. Seeing as we've extensively covered the "self" by now, it's time to address the relationships. Hopefully, throughout your reading experience, you've noticed how many individual factors impact each other. Everything we've discussed in this book affects everything else. And as such, much of what we have already discussed relates to relationships as well. So, to spare the repetition, I implore you to explore how each aspect can also improve your relationships as you work on improving the other aspects of this book.

However, I'd like to dedicate more time to exploring how emotional intelligence can affect our interpersonal relationships. Not only can EI improve our relationships, but it can also help us create new ones and heal broken ones. We were never made to live life alone. Interpersonal relationships are so pivotal to our health, happiness, and survival that finding ways to improve them can be the key to a more fulfilling lifestyle.

RELATIONSHIPS AND EMOTIONAL INTELLIGENCE

There's very little in this life that is better than a relationship that is happy and healthy. However, if you thought that emotional intelligence on a personal level was complex and intricate, imagine managing EI when there are two souls to consider. However complicated it is, emotional intelligence is the key to a happy and healthy relationship. A relationship where each partner recognizes, supports, and cares about the emotions of the other. A relationship where arguments and disagreements are approached with respect, care, and the intent to solve the problem.

However, in the modern era, this is not exactly what everyone is looking for in a relationship anymore. More often, what people are looking for is what Zygmunt Bauman calls "liquid love." Liquid love is described by Bauman (Moore, 2019) as being "loose enough to stop suffocations, but tight enough to give a needed sense of security." In other words, it's a half-love. It's a just-enough love. It's a love that will do for now but that we aren't overly attached to.

As you can imagine, that doesn't lend itself to healthy and fulfilling relationships. Recently, there's been an increased interest in quantity over quality—even in relationships. There's no particular desire for emotional intelligence within relationships anymore. But there should be, and here's why:

- Emotionally intelligent relationships are long-lasting and intimate.
- Both partners in an emotionally intelligent relationship are sensitive toward each other's emotional needs.

- Having an emotionally intelligent relationship motivates us to heartily pursue growth within ourselves and our relationships.
- High emotional intelligence cultivates empathetic connection, commitment, intimacy, and kindness between partners.
- High emotional intelligence helps us avoid those liquid love relationships, prioritizing healthy relationships instead.

HOW TO SPOT AN EMOTIONALLY INTELLIGENT PARTNER

Just as having high emotional intelligence makes you a better partner, a relationship can greatly benefit if the other person in the relationship also has high emotional intelligence. In fact, if you are working on improving your emotional intelligence, your partner may be a great source of inspiration and motivation if they already have high emotional intelligence.

So, how can you spot when your partner has high EI?

- They're great at communicating.
- They're self-sufficient and not emotionally dependent on you or the relationship.
- They're active listeners.
- They are able to remain level headed in stressful situations.
- They are always making an effort to get to know you—they're curious about you.
- They recognize, empathize with, and understand your emotions, as well as their own.
- They're good at "reading the room."

- They're self-aware.
- They have clear and healthy boundaries.
- They have strong, non-romantic, long-lasting relationships.

HOW TO DEAL WITH A PARTNER WHO LACKS EMOTIONAL INTELLIGENCE

Unfortunately, not everyone is lucky enough to find a partner who is emotionally intelligent. Sometimes, we fall in love with someone who can't quite read the room, someone who occasionally lets their emotions get the better of them, or someone who doesn't fully understand our emotions, let alone theirs. I've experienced this personally and can confidently say, "It's no fun."

And that's okay. After all, the heart wants what the heart wants. So, if this is true for you, then how can you manage a relationship with somebody who lacks emotional intelligence, especially when you are on a self-improvement journey?

- Communication. If your partner is not good at picking up on your emotions, then share your emotions with them regularly. Let them know how you feel, and help them understand.

  o Bonus tip: Ask your partner how they best communicate. Adjust accordingly to help them express themselves in their best way.

- Remind your partner that it's you and them against problems and emotions, not you against them. Remind them that you want to work together to improve individually and as a couple.

- Create a safe environment where your partner knows that they won't be misunderstood or invalidated. Remind them that you want to know how they're feeling. Let them know that you expect them to treat you with the same respect.
- Be a good listener when they open up to you. Actively show your interest and desire to get to know them better. Encourage them to talk to you more.
- Start with "yes/no" questions instead of open-ended questions. In the beginning, they may need this extra help to sort out their thoughts and emotions. Don't worry; over time, they will get better at expressing themselves without a helping hand.
- Talk about shared experiences, emotions, opinions, and thoughts. Bond over commonalities.
- Be patient, but persistent. It will take time, and both of you will make mistakes. Be forgiving and open, and encourage your partner to do the same.

TRAUMA AND EMOTIONAL INTELLIGENCE

When we experience trauma, it often leads to a long-lasting effect on our being. Unfortunately, for many, this is as far as the story goes. They experience trauma, and they are forever changed. Often, trauma leaves us with difficulties being empathetic toward others. It leads to harmful and risky behaviors that can further impact our mental and physical health.

However, that does not need to be the end of the story. Healing is possible. Our brains are built to adapt over our lifetimes. Sometimes we cannot control how our brains adapt, but sometimes—with patience, persistence, and care—we can.

This feature of our brains, where neural networks change through growth and reorganization, is called neuroplasticity. Increasing our emotional intelligence changes certain structures within the brain that lead to healing. How? Emotional intelligence increases our ability to manage emotions, conflict, and impulses. Furthermore, emotional intelligence fosters self-awareness, self-confidence, self-compassion, and self-motivation, which are all needed along the healing journey.

Emotional intelligence can also help us minimize the risk of further trauma. We are better equipped to manage conflict, keep a level head, and recognize people who are unhealthy to associate with. Emotional intelligence helps us differentiate between relationships worth mending after trauma and relationships that would only bring about more.

RELEARNING EMOTIONAL INTELLIGENCE AFTER TRAUMA

In her book, *Soul Cry,* Dana Acuri (2020) said, "Healing is like an onion. As you process through one layer of trauma to release the pain and heal, a new layer will surface. One layer after another layer will bring up new issues to focus on."

One of the important layers involved in healing after trauma involves relearning our emotional intelligence. It may feel like a part of us that is eternally broken, but I assure you that it can be mended through effort and dedication. You are worth it, and you can do it.

One way to do so is to address the memory. Often, when we've experienced trauma, that trauma lives on inside of us—as a trigger. When we experience something that reminds us of our trauma to any degree, it can readily bring up the emotions we were feeling in the moment of trauma, even if, currently, we're not in any danger.

Reimmersion is an activity in which we readdress the traumatic event, our memory of it, and the feelings attached to it. The most crucial detail of reimmersion is that it must be done at a healthy and comfortable pace and in a safe place. Reimmersion is a technique used to re-educate the emotional brain and how it responds to and processes the memory of trauma. There are two main ways in which this can happen.

- We can "come to terms" with what happened. In other words, we can acknowledge, accept, and move past what happened to us in the past. We can learn to no longer deny the event or let it define us. We acknowledge and address all the feelings that come with this trauma, and then we let those feelings pass through us. We address it as something significant that happened in our past, but we are now healing and moving on.
- We can "desensitize" ourselves to it. We can minimize the effect triggers have on us. The more we revisit the memory or retell the details, the further distanced we become from the events. "Yes, it happened to us, but now it's just a story I tell." We learn to compartmentalize our emotions in a healthy way.

EMOTIONALLY INTELLIGENT FAMILIES

More often than not, romantic relationships merge into family relationships. This is not the goal for everyone, but after long enough, your partner is your family. And even for those without partners, the vast majority of people have a family unit.

Family is a very large part of being human. Families have existed since the dawn of time, and so have familial problems. Familial problems always seem particularly difficult to resolve because everyone knows each other so deeply that it's easy to bring up soul-crushing ammo.

However, that's not how a family should behave. Just as with every relationship in our lives, we should strive to practice emotional intelligence with our family members to benefit from all the positive ways it can impact the family unit.

These tips are not only for you. Ideally, every member of the family should be putting these tips into practice.

- You are the first step. Make sure that you are actively practicing emotional intelligence. Be a role model for your family. Taking care of yourself is part of emotional intelligence—ensuring that you are levelheaded and emotionally stable.
- Acknowledge your family unit as a team and a collaboration. Don't remain separated from each other. Maintain your individuality, but be active within the family unit.
- Teach emotional choice. Although our emotions seem to take over sometimes, remember that being kind, respectful, and supportive is a choice. Choose right.
- Encourage optimism, but embrace realism. Believe in yourself and in each other.
- Practice what you expect. If you want to be heard, listen. If you want to be motivated, encourage. If you want to be validated, support.
- Encourage individual opinions and values. Don't force the family beliefs on every member. Encourage exploration,

education, and informed decision-making. Offer advice, but don't pressure them in one way or another.

- Communicate. Communicate. Communicate.
- Take responsibility for your nonverbal communication. Don't say you're willing to listen, but spend the entire time turned toward the television. Don't say you're sorry with your fists balled and your teeth clenched.
- Readily acknowledge and address emotions. Name your feelings and triggers.
- Be generous through giving and receiving. Accept gifts, love, and compliments well, and hand them out freely. Practice selflessness.
- Don't problem-solve when it's not needed or asked for. Simply be present, available, and supportive.
- Take the time to get to know each member of your family. Discover their hobbies, likes, and emotional and communicative needs. Learn their love language.
- Take accountability. Don't hide your mistakes—even from the youngsters. Model the behavior of taking accountability and making amends.

For the parents out there, here are a few extra tips on how to practice emotional intelligence, specifically within the realm of the parent-child dynamic.

- Prioritize the connection with your youngster. Don't get distracted by life lessons, discipline, and expectations. The most important thing is continuously learning more about your kid(s) and letting them know you love them.
- Remember that discipline is a teaching tool, not a punishment tool. Discipline is about letting your child(ren) know what you expect from them and allowing them to

learn from their mistakes. Discipline is a tool to enforce boundaries, rules, and limits. Discipline is not a tool to hurt, punish, or degrade your child(ren).

- Practice emotion coaching. Emotion coaching is when you, as the parent, cue your child to practice EI skills such as naming their emotions, naming your emotions, regulating their emotions, and so on. Use big emotions as opportunities to teach and connect. Empower your children.
- Share family values. Ensure that you are actively modeling behavior that aligns with your family values. Explain why each family value is present and why it is important to foster a deep understanding of that value.

WORK RELATIONSHIP WITH EMOTIONAL INTELLIGENCE

Perhaps the only people we spend more time with than our families are our colleagues. And yet, there's often no more than a professional acquaintance-like connection with those at work. But, much like most families, work relationships often produce more stress than fulfillment.

Fortunately, this is not always the case. Some workplaces foster emotional intelligence. Here are some telltale signs that point toward your workplace being an emotionally intelligent environment:

- Low turnover rates. Once employees become a part of the team, they want to stay. People will stick with jobs that leave them emotionally and professionally fulfilled. There are long-term employees who are still passionate about their jobs.

- Everyone openly and freely offers their ideas and input. Employees are not afraid to voice their opinions, even in front of management. Everyone's ideas are respected and acknowledged, even if they're not used in the end.
- Meetings are concise and informative and often contain information that could not have been put in an email. Meetings are held in a way that respects everyone's time, allowing them to get back to work in a timely manner.

If your workplace does not match the points above, it's likely that emotional intelligence is not a priority. However, it's not too late. There are a few ways to encourage emotional intelligence in the workplace.

As a leader:

- Model behavior you'd like to see in the workplace. Demonstrate self-awareness. Talk candidly about your own challenges, weaknesses, strengths, and achievements. Practice self-control.
- Always respond with empathy, support, and understanding. Don't be a pushover, but don't invalidate and ignore your employees.
- Make time for one-on-one meetings to assess your employees' stress levels and emotional state. Don't push for personal information, but try to assess what their overall well-being is.
- Prioritize team-building.
- Communicate. Communicate. Communicate. Ensure that

all lines of communication are efficient, encouraged, and accessible.

As a team member:

- Model the emotionally intelligent behavior previously discussed in this book.
- Part of emotionally intelligent behavior is knowing your limits and not overworking yourself. Maintain your boundaries.
- Readily take accountability for your mistakes, but actively learn from them too.
- Readily forgive team members who make mistakes and assist them in correcting those mistakes.
- Practice and encourage lifelong learning. Take online courses. Constantly improve your skills. Bonus tip: Ask a colleague to take courses with you.
- Engage your colleagues with empathy, understanding, and support.
- Readily express your gratitude toward colleagues and management.

EMOTIONAL INTELLIGENCE IS THE KEY TO A HAPPY RELATIONSHIP WORKSHEET

Regardless of how healthy and emotionally intelligent your relationship is, here are a few questions you and your partner can answer regularly to improve the impact emotional intelligence has on your relationship. You can even use this worksheet with other important people in your life—friends, family, and colleagues.

- What are your relationship goals?

- What do you think your partner's relationship goals are? Compare notes.
- What are three of your core values?
- Are you living according to these values? Can you give an example?
- What are some negative triggers for you (events that trigger negative emotions)?
- How have you communicated these triggers to your partner?
- What are some positive triggers for you (events that trigger positive emotions)?
- How have you communicated these triggers to your partner?
- What things can you change about your environment and experiences that may offer more positive triggers for you and your partner?
- Can you identify a mistake within your relationship?
- Have you corrected this mistake? If not, how can you?
- Let's review your day. Discuss the answers with your partner.

  o What did you spend your time doing?
  o What did you enjoy?
  o What didn't you enjoy?
  o What was the best thing that happened? Why was it the best?
  o What was the worst thing that happened? Why was it the worst?
  o Did you lose your cool at any point in the day?
    ◆ Why?
    ◆ What were the consequences?
  o Did you manage to keep your cool in a stressful situation?

◆ How?

◆ What were the consequences? (Compare these to what the consequences could have been if you had lost your temper.)

○ What would you change about your day if you could?
○ Did you learn anything about yourself today? What was it?
○ Did you learn anything about your partner today? What was it?
○ How did you contribute to your relationship today?
○ How could you have done better today?

- What can you do to improve your mood? Try them out.
- What is a decision you've been struggling with lately?

○ What are your best options? Take this time to choose an option and take action.

- What are three tasks that need to be done but you have not been doing? Do them now, or schedule a time to do them.

BRINGING EMOTIONAL STABILITY IN YOUR LIFE

We're finally nearing the end of this book. Before we continue, I implore you to take a look at where you began and how far you've come. If you've been taking this book one chapter at a time, consider how much you've already grown. If you're reading the whole book before doing any of the activities, then consider all the new information and insight you have.

We're now on the last step—the final topic that we're covering in an attempt to provide you with every tool you need to improve, maintain, and nurture your emotional intelligence. And that topic is creating emotional stability.

Throughout the process of learning about yourself and learning how to identify, understand, and control your emotions, a ton of thoughts and feelings are bound to be stirred up. At this point of the journey, you may already be far more emotionally intelligent, but you may also be struggling with emotional drain and instability.

So, the final step in this book is combating emotional drainage and regaining emotional stability.

SYMPTOMS OF EMOTIONAL DRAIN

You may not even realize that you're emotionally drained. But you are on a journey of self-awareness, so let's take some time to learn what emotional drain feels like and how to identify it in others as well.

Emotional drain, or emotional exhaustion, is when you're feeling worn out or stuck due to the buildup of stress. It can also present as a symptom of burnout. Here's how to know if you are emotionally drained:

- You're lacking motivation.
- You're irritable.
- You're having trouble sleeping.
- You feel absent-minded.
- You're experiencing physical fatigue.
- You're experiencing headaches.
- You don't feel interested in anything.
- You feel anxious.
- There's been a change in your appetite.
- You feel irrationally angry.
- You're having difficulty concentrating.
- You may feel a sense of dread.
- You feel more pessimistic than usual.
- You feel depressed.

HOW TO GET OUT OF AN EMOTIONAL DRAIN

Emotional exhaustion, just like physical exhaustion, is never a good feeling. It doesn't lend itself to growth, happiness, and productivity. It's always in our best interest to reset and reinvigorate ourselves as soon as possible. Here's how you can do that:

- Don't ignore the signs of emotional fatigue. If you notice the signs, take action. Resilience does not include pushing through to your own detriment. Resilience is about recovering. Earlier in this book, we spoke about resilience being measured by the time between distress and recovery. Pushing through will only lengthen that time because you'll have more to mend.
- Maintain a physically healthy lifestyle.

  o Practice healthy sleeping habits. No, this doesn't mean going to bed early and waking up with the sun. There are many different ways to get a healthy amount of sleep in a way that works for you. The most important thing is that you're getting approximately eight hours each day.
  o Practice healthy eating habits. Ensure that your diet is balanced and that you avoid unhealthy things like sugar, processed foods, and caffeine, for example. A balanced diet can offer us necessary vitamins and minerals and can positively affect our digestion and energy levels.
  o Avoid unhealthy substances like drugs and alcohol. On a normal day, it's beneficial to avoid these risky substances, but even more so when we're stressed and emotionally vulnerable.
  o Exercise. You don't have to hit the gym for four hours a day, seven days a week. It's just important to make sure you

move your body every day. There are many ways to do this, some of which can be extremely fulfilling and fun, such as dance classes, swimming, cycling, etc.

- Maintain a mentally healthy lifestyle.

  ○ Focus on the present rather than stressing about the future or ruminating on the past.
  ○ Focus on what you can control and work actively to do so, rather than worrying about things you have no control over.
  ○ Prioritize positive self-talk and minimize negative self-talk.
  ○ Develop and practice all the emotional intelligence skills we've covered in this book.
  ○ Try to maintain a neutral perspective rather than falling strictly on the positive or negative side.

- Practice mindfulness. This involves activities such as:

  ○ journaling
  ○ prayer
  ○ meditation
  ○ breathing exercises
  ○ long walks
  ○ practice gratitude

- Similar to physical exhaustion, sometimes all you need is rest. Take a day for yourself. Watch a comfort movie and practice some self-care. Avoid taking part in emotionally strenuous activities on a daily basis. Allow yourself some time to reset. Take the time to practice your hobbies and partake in leisure activities.

- Use your support system when you need to. Surround yourself with supportive, encouraging, and understanding people. Catch up with them regularly. Talk to them about your problem and consider any advice they give you.
- Seek professional help. Therapy is for everyone. Everyone can benefit from therapy. These professionals can help us with everything in this book and more.
- Don't take on all the responsibility. If possible, delegate tasks to others who are capable so as to not overload yourself with stressors.

ENERGY VAMPIRES

I have a hint to offer you that may help you understand what an energy vampire is:

- If you're emotionally drained, an energy vampire would have nothing to gain from you.

That's right; an energy vampire is someone who—intentionally or unintentionally—drains your emotional energy. You will expend all your energy listening to them, caring for them, giving them advice, empathizing with them, and so on. An energy vampire will leave feeling fresh and satisfied. You will leave feeling overwhelmed and exhausted.

It's important to be able to recognize an energy vampire so as to not fall into their trap. This is how you can spot an emotional vampire:

- You always feel tired or irritable after hanging out with them.
- They're selfish.

- They're usually very charismatic and charming.
- They tend to dominate the conversation.
- They regularly assign blame anywhere but on themselves.
- They're overly dramatic.
- They demand your undivided attention.
- They're manipulative.
- They may lie and cheat regularly.
- They're overly emotional.
- They think and behave erratically.

Types of Energy Vampires

Because they're human beings, energy vampires come in all shapes and sizes. There are six different types of energy vampires.

- The innocent one: Not all energy vampires are always malicious. Innocent vampires are often helpless and are genuinely seeking aid from others, such as children or dependent friends.
- The melodramatic one: These vampires love creating chaos. They feed on drama and use it to fill an underlying emptiness in their lives. They look for opportunities to play the victim but avoid real-life issues.
- The martyr: These vampires feed on your guilt. They feel victimized and personally attacked by others. They regularly assign blame elsewhere and prey on the scapegoat for sympathy.
- The narcissist: They have no empathy or curiosity toward other people. These vampires will always put themselves first. They will manipulate and lie to get what they want.
- The dominator: They love to feel superior and like the most important person in the room. This often stems from an

inner feeling of weakness and inferiority. They usually resort to intimidation tactics.

- The judgmental one: Usually stemming from inner self-worth issues, these vampires thrive on picking on people. They are critical and skeptical.

How to Handle an Energy Vampire

When we're already managing a plethora of our own emotions, as well as the emotions of those we truly care about, the last thing we need is someone taking more than their share of our emotional energy. So, how does one deal with those in our lives who emotionally drain us?

- Establish and enforce boundaries.
- Be on your guard. Energy vampires usually use EI to their advantage. They have the ability to perceive and impact your emotions if you allow them.
- Adjust your expectations, and remember that we cannot change who an energy vampire is. We can only control how we choose to interact with them.
- Don't give an inch, because they will demand a mile.
- In the worst-case scenario, cut off all ties with an energy vampire.

Are You an Emotional Vampire?

Because this book prioritizes self-awareness, it's important to ask this question. Be honest with yourself. Remember, this can be your "before" image, and you can strive to improve yourself. If most of your answers are yes, then you may be an energy vampire.

- Do you feel like

    o people don't understand you or your problems?
    o you have no control over most things in your life?
    o you don't get the attention you require or deserve?
    o everyone has an easier life than you do?
    o you're often helpless, and there are no opportunities to improve yourself and your life?

- Do you regularly need help but feel that no one is willing to offer it?
- Do people regularly complain that you don't listen to them?
- Do you often feel that people don't truly listen to you?
- Do you regularly fight with your friends and family? Is it often their fault?
- Do people often cut ties with you out of the blue?

CREATING AN EMOTIONAL INTELLIGENCE-BASED ENVIRONMENT

We've spent a lot of time working on our emotional intelligence. Would you believe that there is still one more tip I can offer you that can help you along this journey? That tip is to create an environment that encourages emotional intelligence. We've spoken a lot about the things we can and cannot control. Fortunately for us, our environment is often quite comfortably within our control.

If you want to create an environment like this for yourself, schedule the time for self-awareness and reflection. While it is best to do these things daily, tailor it to your own comfort. Make a time to sit down and really assess the time period since you last did this, whether this involves talking out loud, journaling, or simply pondering in silence. Create a list of questions—you can steal from some of the activities in this book—that you can ask and answer each time you do this. You can even track your progress toward self-improvement goals during this time.

If you want to create an environment such as this for those around you (such as colleagues, partners, or even children), here are a few tips:

- Allow them the opportunity to name their emotions. Ask them how they're feeling regularly, and encourage thorough and real answers.
- Provide many opportunities for practicing EI skills such as self-control, adaptability, empathy, social skills, teamwork, and so on.
- Be supportive, encouraging, understanding, and patient.

NEUTRALIZING YOUR EMOTIONS FOR EMOTIONAL STABILITY

The problem with lacking emotional stability is that you are likely to experience more emotional highs and lows rather than having your emotions stay consistent. This constant exaggeration of emotions can quickly drain and overwhelm us. Emotional instability comes from a lack of emotional regulation.

The main method of creating emotional stability is learning how to neutralize your emotions, which essentially means lowering the highs and raising the lows. This does not entail ignoring or invalidating emotions, nor is it the goal to replace one emotion with another. It is merely bringing our emotions to a more manageable level rather than letting ourselves get carried away.

Here are a few tips on how to neutralize your emotions.

- Don't ruminate on the past. Our brain loves to replay events that have upset us in the past and grab onto all those negative emotions. We must train ourselves to leave things that happened in the past in the past because they will only stir up unnecessary emotions.
- Learn to move on. A great way to achieve emotional stability is to focus on the present. Once an event has passed, move on to the next one and focus on it with all your intentions. There are moments of reflection and introspection where events can be revisited, but remember that the purpose of reflection and introspection is to learn or to heal, not to relive and "refeel."
- Practice gratitude. We're always taught to be grateful for people, abilities, and circumstances. While I promote that as well, I do think there is something we regularly forget to be grateful for: our minds and how hard they work to protect us. Thanking your emotions and your triggers is a great way to address them and then move on from them. Furthermore, practice being grateful for even the bad things that happen in life because they bring lessons and growth.
- Forgiveness. Just like holding onto the past, holding onto a grudge only cultivates negative emotions. Sometimes, we're holding a grudge against someone who doesn't even know they've done us wrong and doesn't stand a chance at righting that wrong. Often, holding a grudge causes us more grief than peace. So, work toward forgiveness at every possible opportunity.

FORGIVE YOURSELF

In the previous section, I mentioned that we all needed to practice thanking ourselves more regularly. Along that same note, I'd like to encourage everyone to also explore self-forgiveness. In my own journey, this has been one of the most challenging concepts. We tend to be incredibly hard on ourselves, expecting perfection and holding grudges against ourselves for the smallest infractions.

However, forgiving ourselves is not as easy as saying, "I forgive myself." I know that, for me, it is still incredibly difficult to truly forgive myself. See, genuine self-forgiveness, according to Cornish and Wade (2015), consists of four Rs:

- Responsibility: You must take accountability.
- Remorse: You must work through emotions of shame and guilt.
- Restoration: You must repair relationships and reaffirm values that were broken.
- Renewal: You must learn and grow from the experience.

Self-forgiveness goes a very long way in terms of self-improvement. It is the pinnacle of self-compassion, and it makes it much easier to work in collaboration with ourselves rather than against ourselves. So, how does one achieve self-forgiveness? It's a long and intimate journey, but here are eight steps that you can take:

1. Identify what must be forgiven.
2. Explore accountability. To what extent were you responsible?
3. Accept and explore remorse. Take the time to work through and heal from all the negative emotions that come up.

4. Restore the situation. Make amends where necessary. Re-establish your values.
5. Renewal: Learn from the experience and make choices that won't lead you down this same path in the future.
6. Nurture compassion. Hype yourself up. Be kind to yourself. Remind yourself that you've forgiven yourself.
7. Move on. Now that you've learned from your mistake, there's no longer any reason to dwell on it.

And if it helps any, I forgive you and I believe in you.

Emotional intelligence is the foundation for success in all areas – because everything we do involves interacting with other people. Training ourselves in this area is something we all need, so before you go, take a moment to leave your feedback online to help someone else out.

Simply by sharing your honest opinion of this book and a little about what you found here, you'll inspire new readers to begin their own emotional intelligence journey.

Thank you so much for your support. Emotional intelligence is such an important area to work on for personal growth, and I'm grateful for your support in reaching more people.

CONCLUSION

My deepest desire upon you reading these final pages of *Leveraging Emotional Intelligence* is that you have once again found a sense of self-esteem, joy, and peace. We live in a world where our emotions are constantly on the live wire, and rarely are they given the time, space, and attention to fully recover.

I say that we boycott the comfort people have developed with being emotionally drained. To this world that rings us dry of every molecule of effort and energy we have to offer, I say enough. This started with me, and now I am sharing it with you. One key to over-ruling the world's grip on us is emotional intelligence. We can no longer allow the world to take and take without allowing our bodies the opportunity to refill.

So, if you're tired of being tired—if you've had enough of being overwhelmed and stressed out—I implore you not to forget what you've learned in this book. I implore you to take what you've learned and take the next actionable steps to living an emotionally intelligent life.

I hope that it has become clear to you that understanding our emotions is the foundation for improving every facet of human interaction. Throughout this book, you have become equipped with the tools that are necessary to understand the inner workings of your mind and also to establish deeper, sturdier connections with those you love.

Emotional intelligence is more than just a concept. It's a journey—a journey where we become emotional scientists and learn to use emotions to our advantage rather than getting lost in the whirlwind of feelings. And the destination at the end of this journey is a lifetime of enriched relationships, fulfilling endeavors, and finally, comfort and joy within ourselves.

I have one final activity for you to complete. Use the remaining pages of this book to summarize the most important and impactful lessons you've gained from this book. Should you prefer to invest your future time in learning new skills, I hope that this list acts as a quick reminder to always seek to get to know yourself, to improve yourself, and to thank and forgive yourself.

REFERENCES

Ackerman, C. E. (2018a, February 5). *21 emotion regulation worksheets & strategies.* PositivePsychology.com. https://positivepsychology.com/emotion-regulation-work sheets-strategies-dbt-skills/

Ackerman, C. (2018b, July 3). *What is self-regulation? (+95 skills and strategies).* PositivePsychology.com. https://positivepsychology.com/self-regulation/

Ackerman, C. E. (2018c, July 12). *What is self-acceptance? 25 exercises + definition & quotes.* PositivePsychology.com. https://positivepsychology.com/self-accep tance/#activities-self-acceptance

Aletheia. (2023, September 24). *6 types of energy vampires that emotionally exhaust you.* LonerWolf. https://lonerwolf.com/types-energy-vampire/#h-6-energy-vampire-types

Anderson, N. B., Vice, E., Suzanne Bennett Johnson, Belar, C. D., Breckler, S. J., Nordal, K. C., & Ballard, D. (2011). *Stress in America: Our health at risk.* American Psychological Association. https://www.apa.org/news/press/releases/ stress/2011/final-2011.pdf

Arcuri, D. (2020). *Soul cry.* Dana Acuri.

Ashbaugh, R. (2020, September 23). *6 way to self-soothe when you're feeling triggered.* Solid Foundations Therapy. https://solidfoundationstherapy.com/6-way-to-self-soothe-when-youre-feeling-triggered/

Bailey, C. (2013, October 31). *Why "active listening" will make you more productive, and how to do it.* Chris Bailey. https://chrisbailey.com/active-listening-how-to-do-it/

Bartlett, S. [@StevenBartlett]. (2020, September 30). *There is no self development without self awareness. You can read as many books as you like, but if you're unable* [Tweet]. X (Formerly Twitter). https://twitter.com/StevenBartlett/status/ 1311331455017062406?lang=en

Becker, C. (2021, December 20). *The relation between emotional intelligence and motivation.* Firmbee. https://firmbee.com/emotional-intelligence-and-motivation#thirdparagraph

Birt, J. (2023, February 28). *The importance of emotional intelligence in the workplace.* Indeed Career Guide. https://www.indeed.com/career-advice/career-development/emotional-intelligence-importance

Bisignano, A. (2018, June 1). *Making love last: The importance of emotional intelli-*

gence. Good Therapy. https://www.goodtherapy.org/blog/making-love-last-importance-of-emotional-intelligence-0601184

Bold Creative Life Designs. (2020). *Get motivated worksheet*. Bold Creative Life Designs.https://storage.snappages.site/aq29uwk73d/assets/files/Get-Motivated-Worksheet.pdf

Boogaard, K. (n.d.). *How to foster emotional intelligence in the workplace*. Culture Amp. https://www.cultureamp.com/blog/emotional-intelligence-in-the-workplace

Brackett, M. (2020, January 5). *Become an emotion scientist in 2020*. Marc Brackett, Ph.D. https://www.marcbrackett.com/become-an-emotion-scientist-in-2020/

Bradberry, T. (2022, September 28). *18 signs you have high emotional intelligence*. SUCCESS. https://www.success.com/18-signs-you-have-high-emotional-intelligence/

Brinlee, M. (2021, August 18). *Kristen bell asks her daughters this question when they're dealing with tough emotions*. Romper. https://www.romper.com/entertainment/kristen-bell-daughters-emotional-regulation-strategy

Burton, N. (2018, November 28). *What is intelligence?* Psychology Today. https://www.psychologytoday.com/us/blog/hide-and-seek/201811/what-is-intelligence

Business Management. (2023, March 6). *How do you cope with uncertainty and ambiguity in decision making?* LinkedIn. Retrieved October 16, 2023, from https://www.linkedin.com/advice/0/how-do-you-cope-uncertainty-ambiguity-decision

Cafasso, J. (2023, September 16). *Emotional exhaustion: What it is and how to treat it*. Healthline. https://www.healthline.com/health/emotional-exhaustion#symptoms

ChartWell. (n.d.). *Does emotional intelligence contribute to better health?* ChartWell Blog. Retrieved October 6, 2023, from https://blog.chartwell.com/en/2019/11/does-emotional-intelligence-contribute-to-better-health

Cherry, K. (2021, October 11). *How emotionally intelligent are you?* Verywell Mind. https://www.verywellmind.com/how-emotionally-intelligent-are-you-2796099

Cherry, K. (2022a, November 10). *How psychologists define attention*. Verywell Mind. https://www.verywellmind.com/what-is-attention-2795009

Cherry, K. (2022b, December 1). *The 6 types of basic emotions and their effect on human behavior*. Verywell Mind. https://www.verywellmind.com/an-overview-of-the-types-of-emotions-4163976

Cherry, K. (2023a, March 10). *What is self-awareness?* Verywell Mind. https://www.verywellmind.com/what-is-self-awareness-2795023

Cherry, K. (2023b, May 3). *What is emotional intelligence?* Verywell Mind. https://www.verywellmind.com/what-is-emotional-intelligence-2795423

Cherry, K. (2023c, May 23). *Motivation: The driving force behind our actions*. Verywell Mind. https://www.verywellmind.com/what-is-motivation-2795378

Cherry, K. (2023d, June 29). *Emotions and types of emotional responses*. Verywell Mind. https://www.verywellmind.com/what-are-emotions-2795178

Colorado Network Staffing. (2021, November 5). *7 tips to improve emotional intelligence at work*. Colorado Network Staffing. https://conetstaff.com/%E2%80%8B7-tips-to-improve-emotional-intelligence-at-work/

The Conflict Center. (n.d.). *Expanding your emotional vocabulary*. The Conflict Center. https://conflictcenter.org/expanding-your-emotional-vocabulary/

Connolly, S. (2013, March 4). *5 habits of emotionally intelligent families*. Mental Help.net. https://www.mentalhelp.net/blogs/5-habits-of-emotionally-intelligent-families/

Cornish, M. A., & Wade, N. G. (2015). A therapeutic model of self-forgiveness with intervention strategies for counselors. *Journal of Counseling & Development, 93*, 96–104. https://doi.org/10.1002/j.1556-6676.2015.00185.x

Côté, S., Decelles, K. A., McCarthy, J. M., Van Kleef, G. A., & Hideg, I. (2011). The Jekyll and Hyde of emotional intelligence: Emotion-regulation knowledge facilitates both prosocial and interpersonally deviant behavior. *Psychological Science, 22*(8), 1073–1080. https://doi.org/10.1177/0956797611416251

Cuncic, A. (2023, May 5). *How to develop and use self-regulation in your life*. Verywell Mind. https://www.verywellmind.com/how-you-can-practice-self-regulation-4163536

David, S. (2022, July 20). *Recognizing your emotions as data, not directives*. Susan David. https://www.susandavid.com/newsletter/recognizing-your-emotions-as-data-not-directives/

De La Rosa, B. (n.d.). *How to use emotional intelligence to transform trauma*. https://www.cityofmadison.com/human-resources/documents/Inclusive%20Leadership%20Conf/3_2%20How%20to%20use%20EQ%20Transform%20Trauma.pdf

Del Valle, S. Y., Hyman, J. M., Hethcote, H. W., & Eubank, S. G. (2007). Mixing patterns between age groups in social networks. *Social Networks, 29*(4), 539–554. https://doi.org/10.1016/j.socnet.2007.04.005

Dessen, S. (2012). *Just listen*. Speak.

DiGiulio, S. (2018, August 2). *How to spot (and deal with) an energy vampire*. NBC News. https://www.nbcnews.com/better/health/how-spot-deal-energy-vampire-ncna896251

Doyle, A. (2022, July 7). *What are listening skills?* The Balance. https://www.thebalancemoney.com/types-of-listening-skills-with-examples-2063759

Duncan, C. (2018, March 6). *10 things that steal our motivation—and how to get it back*. Shine. https://advice.theshineapp.com/articles/10-things-that-steal-our-motivation-and-how-to-get-it-back/

Eliot, J. (2015). *Overachievement*. Diversion Books.

Eurich, T. (2018, January 4). *What self-awareness really is (and how to cultivate it)*. Harvard Business Review. https://hbr.org/2018/01/what-self-awareness-really-is-and-how-to-cultivate-it

Farnsworth, B. (2020, April 14). *How to measure emotions and feelings (and the difference between them)*. Imotions. https://imotions.com/blog/learning/best-prac tice/difference-feelings-emotions/

Farrahi, H., Kafi, S. M., Karimi, T., & Delazar, R. (2015). Emotional intelligence and its relationship with general health among the students of University of Guilan, Iran. *Iranian Journal of Psychiatry and Behavioral Sciences, 9*(3). https://doi.org/ 10.17795/ijpbs-1582

Fernández-Abascal, E. G., & Martín-Díaz, M. D. (2015). Dimensions of emotional intelligence related to physical and mental health and to health behaviors. *Frontiers in Psychology, 06*. https://doi.org/10.3389/fpsyg.2015.00317

Foundations Team. (2021, January 22). *Self limiting beliefs and behaviors*. Foundations Asheville. https://foundationsasheville.com/blog/self-limiting-beliefs-and-behaviors/

Gattig, N. (2023, April 27). *18 effective strategies to improve your communication skills*. BetterUp. https://www.betterup.com/blog/effective-strategies-to-improve-your-communication-skills

Giang, V. (2014, October 9). *8 female leaders on how to overcome what's holding women back*. Fast Company. https://www.fastcompany.com/3035478/8-successful-women-leaders-on-how-to-overcome-whats-holding-women-back

Goleman, D. (2013, November 11). *Attention regulates emotion*. LinkedIn. https:// www.linkedin.com/pulse/20131111151023-117825785-attention-regulates-emotion/

Goleman, D. (2020, June 9). *Harvard researcher says the most emotionally intelligent people have these 12 traits. Which do you have?* CNBC. https://www.cnbc.com/ 2020/06/09/harvard-psychology-researcher-biggest-traits-of-emotional-intelli gence-do-you-have-them.html

Grant, A. (2014, January 2). *The dark side of emotional intelligence*. The Atlantic. https://www.theatlantic.com/health/archive/2014/01/the-dark-side-of-emotional-intelligence/282720/

Group Sixty. (2021, January 27). *The enemy within: How to overcome self-limiting beliefs*. Group Sixty. https://www.groupsixty.com/ideas-blog/2021/1/27/the-enemy-within-how-to-overcome-self-limiting-beliefs

Hay Group. (2011). *Emotional and social competency inventory (ESCI) a user guide for accredited practitioners*. http://www.eiconsortium. org/pdf/ESCI_user_guide.pdf

Health Direct. (2022, July). *Motivation: How to get started and staying motivated*. Healthdirect. https://www.healthdirect.gov.au/motivation-how-to-get-started-and-staying-motivated

Herrity, J. (2023, March 11). *10 Ways to develop and improve your social skills*. Indeed

Career Guide. https://www.indeed.com/career-advice/career-development/developing-social-skills

Hislop, A. (n.d.). *The 5 l's of listening and learning...* Mathful Learners. https://mathfullearners.com/the-5-ls-of-listening-and-learning/

Holland, K. (2018, February 13). *How to recognize and respond to energy vampires at home, work, and more.* Healthline. https://www.healthline.com/health/mental-health/energy-vampires

Hugo. (2023, October 15). *11 signs someone has a lack of self-awareness (with examples).* Tracking Happiness. https://www.trackinghappiness.com/signs-lack-self-awareness/

The importance of listening. (n.d.). Github. https://saylordotorg.github.io/text_stand-up-speak-out-the-practice-and-ethics-of-public-speaking/s07-the-importance-of-listening.html

Indeed Editorial Team. (2022a, October 3). *Emotional management skills: What they are and how to develop them.* Indeed Career Guide. https://www.indeed.com/carcer-advice/career-development/emotional-management-skills

Indeed Editorial Team. (2022b, November 24). *What is persuasion? Definition, examples and how it works.* Indeed Career Guide. https://in.indeed.com/career-advice/career-development/what-is-persuasion

Indeed Editorial Team. (2023, September 8). *Social skills: Definition, examples and why they are important.* Indeed Career Guide. https://in.indeed.com/career-advice/career-development/social-skills

Institute for Health and Human Potential. (n.d.-a). *Test your emotional intelligence, free EQ quiz, EI test.* IHHP. https://www.ihhp.com/free-eq-quiz/

Institute for Health and Human Potential. (n.d.-b). *What is emotional intelligence, daniel goleman.* IHHP. https://www.ihhp.com/meaning-of-emotional-intelligence/

invah. (2015, May 27). *10 essential emotion regulation skills for adults.* Reddit. https://www.reddit.com/r/AbuseInterrupted/comments/37gtkv/10_essential_emotion_regulation_skills_for_adults/

Jacob, C. (2023, April 21). *Why are social skills important? - experts' advice.* UpJourney - Live a Happy, Healthy and Successful Life. https://upjourney.com/why-are-social-skills-important

Jain, D. R. (2015). Emotional intelligence & its relationship with life satisfaction. *CENTUM Journal of Management, 8*(1), 61–63. https://doi.org/10.13140/RG.2.1.3693.6802

jimmiedking. (2015, July 8). *Week 23 - BELIEFS, THOUGHTS, FEELINGS, ACTIONS, RESULTS ... make us who we are!* Jimmie D King. Pinterest. https://jimmiedking.com/wellness/beliefs-thoughts-feelings-actions-results-make-us-who-we-are/

Josefowitz, N. (2021, March 8). *3 steps to identify what triggers you.* Psychology

Today. https://www.psychologytoday.com/us/blog/cbt-made-simple/202103/3-steps-identify-what-triggers-you

Jumper. AI. (2021, February 25). *How to win customers with emotional intelligence.* Jumper. AI. https://insights.jumper.ai/how-to-win-customers-with-emotional-intelligence/

Kircanski, K., Lieberman, M. D., & Craske, M. G. (2012). Feelings into words. *Psychological Science, 23*(10), 1086–1091. https://doi.org/10.1177/0956797612443830

La Trobe University. (n.d.). *Why emotional intelligence makes you more successful.* Nest. https://www.latrobe.edu.au/nest/why-emotional-intelligence-makes-you-more-successful/

Laurence, E. (2023, September 4). *What is internal family systems (IFS) therapy?* Forbes Health. https://www.forbes.com/health/mind/what-is-internal-family-systems-therapy-ifs/

Lumen. (n.d.). *What is intelligence?* Lumen. https://courses.lumenlearning.com/waymaker-psychology/chapter/what-are-intelligence-and-creativity/

Manson, M. (2012, March 28). *Are you an emotional vampire?* Mark Manson. https://markmanson.net/are-you-an-emotional-vampire

Marsh, J. (2013, November 14). *Is attention the secret to emotional intelligence?* Greater Good. https://greatergood.berkeley.edu/article/item/is_attention_the_secret_to_emotional_intelligence

Matheka, G. (2021, November 7). *5 psychological habits of people with high self-awareness.* Zeda Magazine. http://www.zedamagazine.com/2021/11/5-psychological-habits-of-people-with-high-self-awareness/

maybeitsmaybelean. (2019, August 9). *Emotional dysregulation has been the hardest part of all this.* Reddit. https://www.reddit.com/r/ADHD/comments/cnxs3z/emotional_dysregulation_has_been_the_hardest_part/?utm_source=share&utm_medium=web2x&context=3

Mayer, J. D., Salovey, P., & Caruso, D. R. (n.d.). *Assess emotional intelligence with ability-based testing.* MHS. https://storefront.mhs.com/collections/msceit

McLaren, K. (n.d.). *Your emotional vocabulary list.* Karla McLaren. https://karlamclaren.com/emotional-vocabulary-page/

Melnke, H. (2019, December 30). *Understanding the stages of emotional development in children.* Rasmussen University. https://www.rasmussen.edu/degrees/education/blog/stages-of-emotional-development/

Meier, J. D. "Emotional Intelligence Quotes to Help You Master Your Emotions." Sources of Insight. Last modified August 3, 2013. https://sourcesofinsight.com/emotional-intelligence-quotes/

Mental Health America. (n.d.). *Helpful vs harmful: Ways to manage emotions.* Mental

Health America. https://www.mhanational.org/helpful-vs-harmful-ways-manage-emotions

Miller, K. (2019, August 20). *50 practical examples of high emotional intelligence.* PositivePsychology.com. https://positivepsychology.com/emotional-intelligence-examples/

Moore, C. (2019, March 19). *Emotional intelligence in relationships - couples activities.* PositivePsychology.com. https://positivepsychology.com/emotional-intelligence-relationships/#happiness-emotional-intelligence-and-our-relationships

Morin, A. (2020, February 5). *12 ways to improve social skills and make you sociable anytime.* LifeHack. https://www.lifehack.org/articles/communication/12-ways-improve-social-skills-and-make-you-sociable-anytime.html

Morin, A. (2021, October 31). *List of feeling words from A to Z.* Verywellfamily. https://www.verywellfamily.com/feelings-words-from-a-to-z-2086647

Motivation Matter. (2020, May 1). *How to use emotional intelligence to boost motivation.* Motivation Matter. https://motivationmatter.com/2020/05/01/how-to-use-emotional-intelligence-boost-motivation/

Mylemarks. (n.d.). *Motivation.* Mylemarks. https://www.mylemarks.com/store/p127/Motivation.html

Nelson, A. (n.d.). *How social leadership is changing the way we lead.* Hppy. https://gethppy.com/leadership/social-leadership-changing

Nguyen, E. (2022, July 14). *How to spot emotional intelligence in a partner.* *Refinery29.* https://www.refinery29.com/en-gb/emotional-intelligence-relationships

Nino-Murcia, A. (2018, December 7). *Emotions are data.* Medium. https://anmcoach.medium.com/emotions-are-data-6960fe87ab4d

O'Bryan, A. (2022, February 8). *How to practice active listening: 16 examples & techniques.* PositivePsychology.com. https://positivepsychology.com/active-listening-techniques/#techniques

Okoronkwo, V. (2022, November 29). *39 best emotional intelligence statistics to know in 2022.* Passive Secrets. https://passivesecrets.com/emotional-intelligence-statistics/

Palbom, K. (2021, December 13). *21 celebrities share their self-care and mental wellness tips.* Slice. https://www.slice.ca/21-celebrities-share-their-self-care-and-mental-wellness-tips/

Pangilinan, J. (2022, August 26). *7 limiting beliefs worksheets that change your thinking.* Happier Human. https://www.happierhuman.com/limiting-beliefs-worksheet/

Paul, M. (2023, January 3). *What emotional triggers are + why you need to understand them.* Mindbodygreen. https://www.mindbodygreen.com/articles/emotional-triggers

Persona Global. (2018, November 29). *Self-Motivation: Building emotional capability.*

Medium. https://medium.com/persona-global/self-motivation-building-emotional-capability-7721891ec0bb

The Personality Lab. (n.d.). *EQ test*. The Personality Lab. https://test2.thepersonality lab.org/eq

Pessoa, L. (2010). Attention and emotion. *Scholarpedia, 5*(2), 6314. https://doi.org/10.4249/scholarpedia.6314

Pisani, H. (2023, June 30). *5 signs you're dating an emotionally intelligent partner*. Truity. https://www.truity.com/blog/5-signs-youre-dating-emotionally-intelligent-partner

PositivePsychology.com. (n.d.). *Graded exposure worksheet*. PositivePsychology.com. https://positive.b-cdn.net/wp-content/uploads/Graded-Exposure-Worksheet.pdf

Psychology Today. (n.d.). *Emotional intelligence test*. Psychology Today. https://www.psychologytoday.com/ca/tests/personality/emotional-intelligence-test

Pyramid Healthcare. (2018, May 28). *Why it is important to have strong social skills and 5 ways to enhance them*. Pyramid Healthcare. https://www.pyramid-healthcare.com/why-it-is-important-to-have-strong-social-skills-and-5-ways-to-enhance-them/

Quora Contributor. (2017, May 23). *How do hormones affect emotions?* Forbes. https://www.forbes.com/sites/quora/2017/05/23/how-do-hormones-affect-emotions/?sh=1aaaedc94275

Raising Children Network. (2021, May 20). *Self-regulation in young children*. Raising Children Network. https://raisingchildren.net.au/toddlers/behaviour/understanding-behaviour/self-regulation

Rankin, L. (2016, April 15). *How to react from a place of love when someone pisses you off*. Mbgmindfulness. https://www.mindbodygreen.com/articles/how-to-react-when-someone-triggers-you

Raypole, C. (2020, November 13). *Emotional triggers: Defintion and how to manage them*. Healthline. https://www.healthline.com/health/mental-health/emotional-triggers

Regan, S. (2021, June 28).*17 social cues, what they mean & how to get better at reading them*. Mbgmindfulness. https://www.mindbodygreen.com/articles/social-cues-types-and-how-to-read-them

Revolution Learning. (n.d.). *The 5 Levels of Listening*. Revolution Learning. https://www.revolutionlearning.co.uk/article/the-5-levels-of-listening/

Riopel, L. (2019, September 14). *17 self-awareness activities and exercises (+ test)*. PositivePsychology.com. https://positivepsychology.com/self-awareness-exercises-activities-test/

Rizzo, A. (2021, November 22). *Self in IFS therapy - what it is, what are the 8 c's and the 5 p's of self*. Therapy with Alessio. https://www.therapywithalessio.com/articles/self-in-ifs-therapy-what-it-is-what-are-the-8-cs-and-the-5-ps-of-self

Schell, A. (2022, April 28). *Intrinsic motivation - leader EQ*. Dr Andy Schell CPA. https://www.doctorschell.com/post/intinsic-motivation

Scott, J. (2012). *Clear: A guide to treating acne naturally*. CreateSpace Independent Publishing Platform.

Segal, J. (2023a, October 11). *Emotional intelligence in love and relationships*. HelpGuide.org. https://www.helpguide.org/articles/mental-health/emotional-intelligence-love-relationships.htm

Segal, J. (2023b, October 11). *Tips to improve family relationships*. Help Guide. https://www.helpguide.org/articles/mental-health/improving-family-relationships-with-emotional-intelligence.htm

Shanti-Som Wellbeing Retreat. (2023, July 8). *Emotional intelligence and happiness*. Shanti-Som. https://www.shantisom.com/en/blog/emotional-intelligence-and-happiness/

Shetty, J. (2020, August 25). *Jay shetty on how motivations reveal your true intentions*. Jay Shetty. https://jayshetty.me/blog/jay-shetty-on-how-motivations-reveal-your-true-intentions/

Skilled at Life. (n.d.). *How beliefs are formed and how to change them*. Skilled at Life. https://www.skilledatlife.com/how-beliefs-are-formed-and-how-to-change-them/

Skills You Need. (n.d.). *What is communication? Verbal, non-verbal & written*. Skills You Need. https://www.skillsyouneed.com/ips/what-is-communication.html

Stanborough, R. J. (2021, January 25). *EQ vs IQ: How they differ, which is more important?* Healthline. https://www.healthline.com/health/eq-vs-iq#is-one-more-important

Steiner, C. (1979). *Healing alcoholism*. Grove Press.

Stern, O. (2021, March 29). *What to do if you think your partner lacks emotional intelligence*. Thrive Global. https://community.thriveglobal.com/what-to-do-if-you-think-your-partner-lacks-emotional-intelligence/

Suleman, Q., Syed, M. A., Mahmood, Z., & Hussain, I. (2020). Correlating emotional intelligence with job satisfaction: Evidence from a cross-sectional study among secondary school heads in khyber pakhtunkhwa, pakistan. *Frontiers in Psychology, 11*. NCBI. https://doi.org/10.3389/fpsyg.2020.00240

Szekely, G. (2023, September 15). *How to deal with a partner who lacks emotional intelligence*. The Couples Center. https://www.thecouplescenter.org/how-to-deal-with-a-partner-who-lacks-emotional-intelligence/

Team Asana. (2023, January 3). *10 limiting beliefs and how to overcome them*. Asana. https://asana.com/resources/limiting-beliefs

Team Stage. (n.d.). *23+ monumental motivation statistics for 2021*. TeamStage. https://teamstage.io/motivation-statistics/

Tenney School. (2017, February 22). *Learning environments that stimulate emotional intelligence*. Tenney School. https://tenneyschool.com/learning-environments-that-stimulate-emotional-intelligence/

Therapy with Abby. (n.d.). *How to cope with being triggered*. Therapy with Abby. https://www.therapywithabby.co.uk/blog/how-to-cope-with-being-triggered

throwaway4rltnshp. (2021, December 5). *Life transformation: Overcoming limiting beliefs and redefining oneself (a case study)*. Reddit. https://www.reddit.com/r/lawofattraction/comments/r9q1fg/life_transformation_overcoming_limiting_be liefs/?utm_source=share&utm_medium=web2x&context=3

Tiwari, D. (2022, January 25). *17 tips to recover from feeling emotionally drained*. Choosing Therapy. https://www.choosingtherapy.com/emotionally-drained/

Vanzant, I. [@IyanlaVanzant]. (2017, February 9). *Everyone comes into our lives to mirror back to us some part of ourselves we cannot or will not see* [Tweet]. X (Formerly Twitter). https://twitter.com/IyanlaVanzant/status/829736630223134721

WebMD Editorial Contributors. (n.d.). *What is emotional dysregulation?* WebMD. https://www.webmd.com/mental-health/what-is-emotional-dysregulation

Well+Good Editors. (2023, September 13). *If marathon season has you feeling inspired to run, these are the essentials experienced runners say you need to get started*. Well+Good. https://www.wellandgood.com/running-essentials-nike/

WFU Online Counseling. (n.d.). *The difference between feelings and emotions*. WFU Online Counseling. https://counseling.online.wfu.edu/blog/difference-feelings-emotions/

Wignall, N. (2020a, February 17). *5 habits of highly self-aware people*. Nick Wignall. https://nickwignall.com/self-aware-people/

Wignall, N. (2020b, October 9). *6 signs of low self-awareness*. Nick Wignall. https://nickwignall.com/6-signs-of-low-self-awareness/

Wignall, N. (2021, November 4). *10 simple ways to improve your self-awareness [with examples]*. Nick Wignall. https://nickwignall.com/self-awareness/

Wood, K. (n.d.). *Increasing your emotional intelligence | Introduction to body scanning*. Kamini Wood. https://www.kaminiwood.com/introduction-to-body-scanning-boosting-emotional-intelligence/

Woods, S. C. (2018). *Are you aware of your self-limiting beliefs?* Truist Leadership Institute. https://www.truistleadershipinstitute.com/publications-research/media-publications/are-you-aware-of-your-self-limiting-beliefs

Wooll, M. (2022, July 19). *Don't let limiting beliefs hold you back. Learn to overcome yours*. BetterUp. https://www.betterup.com/blog/what-are-limiting-beliefs

Workplace Strategies for Mental Health. (2022, August 9). *The function of emotions*. Workplace Strategies for Mental Health. https://www.workplacestrategiesformental health.com/resources/the-functions-of-emotions

Worldometer. (2023). *World Population Clock*. Worldometer. https://www.worldome ters.info/world-population/